PAID IN FULL

The Story
of Harold Ryckman
Missionary Pioneer
to Paraguay and Brazil

by Lucile Damon Ryckman

LIBRARY
BRYAN COLLEGE
DAYTON, TN. 37321

Light and Life Press
Winona Lake, Indiana 46590

64504

All rights reserved. No part
of this book may be reproduced in any form,
except for brief quotations in reviews, without
the written permission of the publisher.

Copyright © 1979 by
Light and Life Press

Printed in the United States of America
by Light and Life Press,
Winona Lake, Indiana
46590   ISBN 0-89367-033-2

Dedication

To our missionary colleagues
and national pastors
in Paraguay and Brazil,
this book is lovingly dedicated.

Table of Contents

Acknowledgments

I acknowledge my indebtedness to the Lord who gave me courage to continue with research and writing.

To the following friends I also express my deep appreciation: to Dr. Byron S. Lamson for editing the manuscript; to LeOra Mudge and Mary Newland for their suggestions and encouragement; to Dr. Lamson and Dr. John Mizuki for permission to quote from their books; to Marian Groesbeck for permission to use material formerly printed in the *Missionary Tidings;* to William Kettenring for typing the final draft; to the Reverend and Mrs. Donald Bowen for help in collecting the photographs.

I also am grateful to all my friends who have supported me with their love and prayers.

Preface

The United Nations was organized in 1945. There was a great upsurge of world concern in North America. This new national interest in world affairs certainly influenced the churches of our nation. The number of overseas missions reported in 1919 by fifteen mission boards totaled 6,087. In 1948 that number had fallen to 5,192. A sense of urgency regarding the world mission of the church was experienced by many denominations. By 1964 there were 43,000 Protestant missionaries in the world, and church leaders were challenging their people for more generous contributions and even larger commitment of personnel.

Free Methodists were caught up in the spirit of the times. Between 1944 and 1960, ten new mission fields were established. Membership in our overseas churches increased more than 500 percent, and the number of our missionaries quadrupled. The Latin American story is part of this epic advance.

In Africa, the pioneer work of opening new fields was usually a cooperative venture by national church leaders and experienced missionaries. Often, the same language was used on the new field which was frequently the natural expansion of an existing conference. Not so in South America.

Attempts to transfer Portuguese-speaking missionaries to Brazil were unsuccessful. Spanish-speaking leaders from our Latin missions in California were not available. But read this story, an eye-witness account, lovingly written and factually reliable. There is careful research and a generous use of official correspondence, diaries, and board meeting minutes along with supporting data from missionary colleagues.

It is a moving story. Here are devoted people with no previous missionary experience and without benefit of counsel from older workers, attempting to lay the foundations of the mission and church on a continent heretofore untouched by Free Methodism. Harold Ryckman was the pioneer leader in this advance.

I have been in tears time and again reading this very human document. My admiration for a long-time friend, the Reverend Harold Ryckman, has been heightened. The "real" Harold still seems beyond our grasp. This man of great faith and vision was an efficient organizer and administrator. He was an outstanding preacher of the gospel, equally fluent in Spanish, Portuguese, and English.

At the same time, he drew from earlier experiences as a manual arts teacher. He was the builder-contractor for the extensive building programs required on a new field. He was a careful planner, a thoughtful businessman. He counted Brazilians and Japanese as colleagues. They worked together as a team. The missionary secretary made no visits to this field to deal with "an emergency."

The shadow of this great man falls across my life. It was easy to confide in him, to bare my soul. We were "brothers" in the family of God. It seemed to me that it was a rather special arrangement — that I was sort of on the inside, and I was. He never betrayed this confidence. But now I find that others felt the same way. This man just put people absolutely first in his life. He was "full of faith" in people, urging scholarships for young people, and a second chance for the ones who failed. God bless his influence. I want to be on the same street with him in heaven.

Byron S. Lamson

Introduction

Harold Ryckman looked into the barrel of the large revolver as the officer demanded his car, his keys, and his documents of identification.

Others yelled, "Communists! Kill that one! He owns the place!"

A new dictator-president had come to power through a military coup. Unrest pervaded the tiny landlocked country of Paraguay. Big-neighbor Brazil was hunting communists among retired army officers, while the United States was losing battles to the communists pouring into South Korea. The dominant religion of Latin American sought to maintain the status quo and often spread the rumor that North American missionaries were "communist agents."

Such a dramatic confrontation with the authorities was a new experience for the tall, slender North American in his fifth year as missionary to Paraguay. Here is his modest account of that incident:

"Not all is dull and routine on the mission field. Exciting experiences come at times. And so it happened suddenly on a Sunday afternoon in November. Quite often a group of young men from the church goes out on Sundays to visit in the homes of the people and spread the gospels and tracts. This Sunday afternoon we went, together with a girl of twelve years and her father. I was surprised at the father taking the girl but said nothing. Later, I discovered that the Lord was preparing a path ahead of us.

"We were going to visit in a new community about ten miles distant from the mission compound. One of the young men, a recent convert, lived there and had already sold a number of Bibles to his neighbors and friends. They were asking that we come and explain more fully the way of salvation. When we arrived at the home of this young man, he went out to call his friends. But soon he returned saying that none were home. We visited for a while, had a season of prayer, and started to return home.

"As we arrived at the front gate we were met by two men in plain clothes, one of them with a revolver in his hand. He demanded our documents and the keys to the station wagon. I said, 'What is this, the law?' They replied, 'Yes.' And almost at once, others arrived yelling, 'Beat them! Kill them! Kill that one, he owns the place!'

"The head of the party told one of the others, 'Over there in that clump of trees are the police. Go and call them!' In a few minutes they came — four with rifles, and an officer with a revolver in his hand.

"I was sure there was some mistake, so as they approached I stepped forward to explain to the officer that we were simply evangelical missionaries and that they were arresting innocent people. But instead of answering, he started beating me across the back with a horsewhip. When I asked him why he was doing this, he pointed his revolver at me as if to shoot. Our pastor, the Reverend Mr. Palella, felt certain he was going to kill me. But, after that, he turned on the others and, one by one, practically all were whipped.

"In the meantime, one of the police had examined our documents and announced that I was a North American and that Mr. Palella was an Argentinian and to be careful how they treated us. The officer apologized to me for the beating and placed us, together with the girl, aside under the guard of one of the police. The others were forced to return into the house which was then thoroughly examined. Here they forced all the Paraguayan young Christians to pick up heavy objects, benches, chairs, books, earthen jars, and so forth, and to carry them on their backs. We were all marched five miles, to the nearest police station. The officers and men, all who could get in, rode in the Chevrolet.

"As we walked we had opportunity to testify to the guards who accompanied us. One young man said, 'I carry but a bench on my back; Jesus carried the cross for me. I have received but a few lashes. Jesus suffered to the death for me.' A real joy welled up in our hearts to be counted worthy to suffer something for Him who gave *all* for us. As we passed along, the people jeered, 'Ah, los evangelicos!'

"One of the guards said, 'We were told that you were communists, but we see that you are not. What are you?' We had opportunity on that trip to explain the gospel to several who had never heard before and perhaps would never have heard it in any other way. Upon arriving at the police station two hours later, we were booked as prisoners and placed in the inner patio. There also we had opportunity to preach the love of Jesus to both officers and prisoners.

"We remained there until dark, when we were told that we were to be taken to Asunción where we would have to be examined by the Department of Investigations. We were crammed into our station wagon and taken there. Again, we were carefully searched and booked and placed in the inner patio. No accusations had been made as yet, and we were beginning to feel that we were getting to be rather embarrassing to them because we were continually testifying of the goodness of God and of His love for all mankind. They were forced to admit that the spirit of Christ was being shown by the 'evangelicos.'

"Many now were asking us about our beliefs and our religion. 'Just where is your church? This must be a good religion which you are teaching.' We heard others say, behind our backs, 'These people certainly are acting courteously. They are really gentlemen.' One of the prisoners said to another who was using profanity, 'You will have to quit that here now. We have some people of culture with us.' During that night, until 2:00 A.M., there was a group of prisoners sitting around listening to one or the other of the evangelicals tell of the great salvation that Jesus alone can give.

"It was here that we began to realize that the Lord had foreseen our plight and had prepared the way before us. When they were placing us in the jail for the night, the father of the girl said, 'Surely you will not put this innocent girl in there with all these men.' They permitted him to step to one side with her and wait. Up to this point we had not been permitted to call or advise any of our people of our arrest, although it was now 9:00 P.M. and we were to have been back for the service at 7:00 P.M. I was called out front again at 9:30 and advised that the father of the girl was going to take her out to our place to stay for the night, that an officer would accompany them and bring the father back. Her father said, 'I will try to advise our people as to our predicament and, if possible, bring some blankets so we can get some rest tonight.'

"As they were passing the Baptist church, where the meeting was just ending, he got a sudden impression to say, 'Here, this is the place.' They stopped, he took the girl inside and left her in care of some of the women. He also explained our situation, then returned to the street. But the police car had gone and he was free! He boarded a streetcar and went at once to advise an American missionary, a Baptist M.D., who, in turn, advised the American Embassy.

"At 10:30 I was called to the front again. I was met by the American consul who was demanding my release. It was granted, and I walked out to the street with him. After riding in his car to the Embassy, I found waiting for me the father of the girl and Dr. Fowler, the Baptist M.D. We went at once to the Argentine Embassy with the hope of securing the release of our pastor, Mr. Palella. But it was now late, and although we tried until after midnight,

14

we did not succeed. Then we went to our mission and told our story to those anxiously waiting to hear what had happened to us. I took blankets to those in the jail and left them for the night. At 6:00 the next morning I was on hand again with a hot breakfast for the Christians.

"At 8:00 A.M., when the chief of the department arrived, the president of the Central Committee of Evangelicals, Dr. Reinaldo Decoud, was there, too, to protest. But there was also much indignation among the officials of the police. All the evangelicals were given their liberty at once, except the owner of the house in the country. He was kept until later in the day for further examination, then he, too, was given his liberty. We visited the chief of police and other heads of departments and were graciously received. They promised to intervene in prevention of that type of action in the future and promised us protection. So, we 'departed from the presence of the council, rejoicing that we were counted worthy to suffer shame for His name.'

"We are now well acquainted with the authorities and they with us, which may prove to be a real asset in the future. But most of all, our own spirits have been quickened and proved. We are now willing to give ourselves more fully to Him who died to save us."

* * *

This "prisoner of the Lord" became my husband in 1966. Late in 1977 I accepted the invitation to write a short book focusing on Harold and his pioneer missionary work in Paraguay and Brazil.

Harold brought in the big cardboard boxes of files dating back to 1946, the year he went to South America. We were planning the project together. Then came the big shock! Harold had an acute heart attack on January 5, 1978. He was in and out of the hospital three times. In his sleep at home, in the wee hours of a February morning, his spirit slipped away to be with Jesus.

This is not a comprehensive history of Free Methodist

missions and churches in Paraguay and Brazil. Our dear friends and co-workers, Japanese, Brazilians, Paraguayans, and North Americans — too numerous to name — have had a vital part in such a history.

I have been asked to tell the Harold Ryckman story. He was Free Methodism's pioneer missionary to Paraguay. I want you to see his commitment to Jesus Christ, his concern for the spiritually blind, his love for his fellow workers, and the effectiveness of his influence in the planting of churches in Paraguay and Brazil.

Harold and Evalyn Ryckman were appointed to Paraguay in October, 1945. Helen Voller and Lucile Damon were appointed to Brazil. Helen and I had been students together in Greenville College.

Helen was an elementary schoolteacher. For several years she was a full-time children's evangelist in the East Michigan Conference. When the Lord called me to South America, I was secretary to Mr. B. H. Gaddis, publishing agent at Free Methodist headquarters. I had taught in high schools in Wisconsin where my father was a pioneer Free Methodist minister.

During their first term in South America the Ryckmans lived in Asunción, the capital of Paraguay. From 1952 to 1962 their base of operation was in Brazil, and Harold was superintendent of both fields.

In 1962 Harold became the first executive secretary of the World Fellowship of Free Methodist Churches. His office was at Winona Lake, Indiana. From there he visited our churches and conferences in Africa, Hong Kong, Taiwan, Japan, the Philippines, and Ireland. While they were living in Winona Lake, Evalyn went to be with the Lord.

After organizing the World Fellowship office and its work, Harold turned to the important task of Area Secretary for Latin America. He moved to Ontario, California, and went to the Latin fields as the needs demanded. In July of 1966 he returned to Brazil with a

16

VISA crusade. Staying on after the crusade, Harold decided to ask me to become his wife. In December of that year, we were united in a simple and beautiful ceremony in the Winona Lake Free Methodist Church. Our loving Heavenly Father blessed us with more than eleven years of a perfect marriage.

In the following pages I have chosen to draw heavily upon Harold's own writings and excerpts from his letters. Many of the latter were written to Dr. Byron S. Lamson, missionary secretary during the first eighteen years of our missionary life, and our highly esteemed friend.

Chapter 1

Before the Beginning

Among Harold's papers I found the beginning of an autobiography.

"I was born many years ago, back in the smallest numbers of the twentieth century, in the north central part of the United States (Dale, North Dakota), where the winters were cold, sometimes down to forty-five or fifty degrees below zero. The snow would be on the ground all winter, at times as much as eight or ten feet deep. We lived far enough north that many times we could see the northern lights dancing in the sky.

"My father was a farmer with about six hundred acres of land, received through a government grant. My first winter on this earth was spent, so I am told, in a sod house made out of the soil through which millions of grass roots had grown, holding it together. Chunks of this, which looked like large bricks, were cut out of the ground to form the walls. Then it was plastered and whitewashed within and became a very warm and comfortable abode. The next year the frame house was built.

"I had one brother two years older than I and another five and a half years younger. My older brother, Ernie, led me into many interesting and exciting adventures. Especially do I remember sliding downhill on our sleds and ice-skating on the pond.

"I recall with great pleasure the cold winter evenings when I was five or six years old and my father would read Bible stories and explain them to us. Then we would all kneel and pray to our Heavenly Father. What a blessed heritage God gave me. This was worth many times more than great wealth or a great name.

"But this blessed privilege soon became a pressing responsibility upon me. Before I was very old, the enemy of souls brought many wicked temptations before me and it was not long until I was yielding to them. After that, it wasn't as easy to pray and listen to the reading of the Bible. My heart was heavy and sad. Many times at the family altar I confessed out my wrong doings and asked God to forgive me, which He always freely did. Then was restored to me the joy and contentment which I had known.

"When I was eight years old my father sold the farm rather suddenly and announced that we were going to move. He felt God was calling him to preach the gospel, and he was going to prepare. We moved to California where he entered a Bible school in Los Angeles. During one year he worked hard and made good grades. Then sickness came upon him and he was forced to quit.

"When I was twelve, we moved to a little farm near Chino, where my father hoped to regain his health. He was reasonably well. I remember him most clearly during those days. I think he was the most joyful man in spiritual matters I ever knew. I knew it was the joy of the Lord. But I was entering adolescence and wasn't as free to talk out my spiritual needs as before. There were long periods when my heart condemned me. At last I gave up and quit trying to be a Christian. Many times I had a great desire to be saved but would not confess it to others. My parents were wise in dealing with me. Instead of doing too much talking, they spent much time and effort in praying for me. My older brother was, I think, in about the same condition as I. We worked hard on the farm and went to high school. Both of us were so busy with school and farm work that we were too tired or too occupied to be very serious about spiritual things.

"My father took very ill again when I was fourteen, and in less than a year he passed away. He knew he was not going to live. He faced death fearlessly, making every preparation he possibly could. Many times at the family altar he talked of his being ready, even eager, to go and be with his Saviour. His steady assurance in Christ has always stayed with me. I have never doubted the reality of salvation after seeing the sustaining confidence with which my father came down to death. After his death, our work became even harder. While I always attended Sunday school and church, yet I was in darkness in my soul.

"When I was seventeen years of age I had a spiritual awakening. There were special evangelistic services in our church (Chino Free Methodist). My mother urged me to seek the Lord. I went forward one night and tried to pray. But I couldn't. Heaven's doors seemed closed. I pleaded but got no answer. Then I really became alarmed. Years before, there had been times when conviction had come to my heart and I felt a strong urge to confess my sinful ways and repent and turn to God. But I had no such feeling now. It was simply a feeling of fright and hopelessness. One night when I was praying, I promised God that if He would let conviction come back to me I would at once yield to Him. I was really in earnest. It was several months before God answered my prayer.

"One night in the church service God spoke once more to my heart. I was prepared and kept my promise. When the invitation was given, I went forward and knelt at the altar. There God helped me to pray as I had not prayed in years. There were real tears of confession and repentance. There were some people whom I had wronged, and I asked their forgiveness. There were some confessions I had to make by mail. I promised to make them. I really surrendered to God that night."

At this point, Harold's autobiography ends. But in our

years together he talked often of his youth. After high school, he worked for three years in construction, learning the building and cabinet-making trades. His great desire was to be an engineer. California School of Technology accepted him, but before he could enter, God clearly indicated Los Angeles Pacific College. There the Holy Spirit pressed upon him a call to preach. A deep inner struggle ensued.

"But Lord, You know how timid and shy I am. Why, I could never preach!" he said.

The Lord whispered, "Can't you trust me?"

In Harold's mind, he thought he might be able to pastor one of the smallest churches in the conference, with the Lord's help, but never anything more. He began to prepare for the ministry. After two years at Los Angeles, he went to Greenville College, graduating in 1927.

That fall he and Evalyn Bartholomew were married in the Chino Free Methodist Church. Evalyn was a dedicated Christian and they had been sweethearts for many years.

Harold taught at the Boys' Junior Republic and Evalyn was a county nurse. In 1929 he was appointed pastor of the San Bernardino Free Methodist Church. Trusting God to supply their needs in those Depression days, they gave up their secular employment to devote their complete time to the church. Their salary was seventeen dollars a week. They served churches at Pomona, Santa Monica, and Whittier, California, and at Phoenix, Arizona. In Phoenix they started three Sunday schools which became self-supporting churches. Harold was superintendent of the Arizona district. He pioneered the opening of the church in Prescott, along with his district responsibilities. After seventeen years in the pastoral ministry, Harold's life had a new beginning.

Chapter 2

Doors Open
to South America

Roots of the Free Methodist Church
in South America go back to Japan. Early in the
twentieth century, immigrants from crowded Japan had
sought new opportunities in Brazil. In 1927, Yoshitaro
Fugita, a Free Methodist colporteur in Japan, came with
his family to the state of Sao Paulo. A year later, Daniel
Nishizumi, a graduate of the Osaka Free Methodist
Seminary, arrived. There he met the Fugita family and
later married their daughter, Yoshie.

Not until 1934 did the Free Methodist dentist,
Hiroyuki Hayashi, and his little family reach Brazil. In
the city of Sao Paulo, Nishizumi and Hayashi met,
became friends, and agreed to work together in establish-
ing a Free Methodist church. On November 1, 1936, with
twenty-one people attending the meeting, the little church
came into being. The following year three preaching
points were opened.

In 1938, Nishizumi went to the United States and
Japan. While in the States he talked with the missionary
secretary, the Reverend Harry Johnson, asking for
missionaries. As a result of his fervent missionary appeal
in Japan, two couples, the Seiti Simizus and the Sukeichi
Onos, answered the call. None of these Japanese
missionaries had any financial support from the Japanese
church. They did have their blessing and prayers.

In the meantime, the Free Methodist Church in North
America had a concern for missions in South America. In
1940, Harry Johnson, B. H. Pearson, and E. E. Shelhamer

made a survey trip to the southern continent. As a result, the Commission on Missions voted to open work in Sao Paulo. They also approved purchasing the Good Samaritan Orphanage in Asunción. Missionaries were appointed to both fields, but passports were denied. All was at a standstill.

After the end of the war in 1945 the new missionary secretary, the Reverend Byron S. Lamson, went to Washington, D.C., to confer with the state department regarding passports for South America. He received a favorable reply. A search for personnel followed. The secretary contacted Harold and Evalyn Ryckman.

I have heard Harold give his testimony many times of the events which followed. He would say:

"When Evalyn and I were approached about going to South America, I had a real problem. I enjoyed the pastorate. I could not understand that it would be God's will to leave it. Evalyn, though, had felt a call to the mission field from her childhood.

"We began to seek God's will in earnest. One day I said to her, 'I think we just better forget about this letter from Brother Lamson. I believe God wants us to stay in the pastorate.' Her reply was, 'I think you need to pray some more.'

"I went to my study to pray. The Lord gave me these words from Acts 5:38, 39: 'If this counsel or this work be of men, it will come to nought: but if it be of God, ye cannot overthrow it; lest haply ye be found even to fight against God.' "

At this point Harold wrote Dr. Lamson:

"We have received your two very exciting letters. . . . We have been praying for a definite answer from the Lord regarding His will. . . . I am in serious doubt that Evalyn is in physical shape to go. . . . That in itself may be the barrier which keeps me from feeling definitely that this is God's will. . . .

24

"I feel to say, after much prayer, that if God is leading in this direction, He will open the way. . . . God knows that it is my utmost desire to be used however and wherever I can be the most use in His work. Sacrifice means nothing to me. Loneliness and separation from the folks here I will gladly endure. I anticipate the thrill of the adventure and the joy of bringing the true gospel message to those who have never heard. . . . My heart is in it. Should the steps leading up to our going all work out, . . . you may be assured that I will not shrink from the task.

"Yes, we will be ready for appointment to Paraguay providing God continues to lead. This is a great step for us, as it will change the whole remainder of our lives and of our son's life. We must be certain that it is in God's plan. That is all. You would want that, too."

They went to Winona Lake for the October Board meeting. It was then I first became acquainted with the Ryckmans. They were appointed to Paraguay, subject to Evalyn's passing a final physical examination. To Harold's surprise, she passed. Esther Harris from Washington, and Ruth Foy from Pennsylvania, were also designated for Paraguay.

True to Harold's word, there was no "shrinking back" once the decision was made. In early April, Harold and Evalyn and twelve-year-old Donald said good-bye to family and friends and boarded the train in Alhambra, California, for New Orleans where they had reservations on a freighter. In Louisiana, they encountered a long, frustrating delay. It was not until May 19 that they finally sailed from Houston. Later, they understood God's timing.

In the meantime, Helen Voller and I left New York on a Norwegian freighter. A heavy fog hung like a blanket over our ship on the first day. During our early evening meal we suddenly heard the blast of a ship's horn. Greatly startled, I jumped from my chair and ran to the nearest porthole. What I saw sent cold shivers up and down my back. On our left was a huge ship. "This is it!" I said to myself. "There will not even be time to find a life jacket!" But miraculously, so the captain said, we escaped collision.

Several letters awaited us when we arrived in Rio de Janeiro, the most beautiful harbor in the world. One was from the Reverend Daniel Nishizumi in Sao Paulo — two hundred seventy miles southwest — informing us that the Ryckmans were in Rio. Imagine their surprise to see Helen and me sitting in the lobby of their small hotel when they returned from a sightseeing trip! Eating dinner together, we had a delightful time recounting our experiences. Helen and I were introduced to the Brazilian *cafezinho ("demitasse")*. Harold never ceased to enjoy describing Helen's facial expression when she tasted the coffee for which she had refused sugar.

The Ryckmans left by air the next morning for Sao Paulo where they spent a few days with the Japanese Free Methodists before going to Asunción. Our ship departed two days later for Santos, port of Sao Paulo.

Chapter 3

First Impressions

What were Harold's reactions to South America? Tucked away in his file I found the following writing, entitled "First Impressions." The edges are tattered and the paper is yellowing with age.

"It was in June of 1946 when the freighter *Victory*, after thirteen days en route from Houston, finally pulled into the harbor of Rio de Janeiro. It was 6:00 A.M. We were all planning on seeing the sights. We were not yet accustomed to the *mañana* speed of Latin America. We docked at 6:00 P.M. just after dark.

"We did manage to get off the ship at 8:00 P.M. Since this was our port of disembarkation, we wanted to find a hotel as quickly as possible. A traveling friend, who spoke some Portuguese, accompanied us. Seeking a telephone we entered a *bar* (a quick lunch place with wide, wide doors, always open onto the street.) I was not accustomed to entering "bars." Was there not a better place? Upon entering, I saw men standing in front of a long marble counter, each with a tiny cup in front of him. Some were filling the cup with sugar. What was this? Soon a waiter came and poured coal-black liquid on top of the sugar. The men hastily took it all down with a swallow or two and quickly went out. 'What kind of whiskey was this?' I asked my friend.

"Hotel rooms were scarce, but one was finally located through the YMCA. We got into a taxi, the driver was given the address of the hotel, we said good-bye to our friend, and we were on our own. Arriving at the hotel, we were taken to our room by a porter who did not speak English. Later, we found that no one in the hotel spoke English. It was swim or drown! We looked forward to a good hot shower and a comfortable bed. The shower wasn't so 'hot' and the beds were less than comfortable.

"Then came morning. Breakfast? I would go and explore. The dining room was abandoned. Evidently, from all I could decipher, we were to be served in our rooms. I could hardly wait. Ham and eggs? Or perhaps hotcakes? It proved to be *café* (coffee). Coal-black liquid. I didn't know how to tell the waiter to stop pouring. In fact, I was accustomed to a full cup of coffee with a bit of cream. He filled my cup more than three-fourths full and then added hot milk. It was as bitter as it looked. Then came bread — hard, dry, and dark. Those were the days of almost no white flour in Brazil. There was butter. And that was it!

"We spent five days in Rio, and we gradually caught on. Rio de Janeiro is a beautiful city, but how to see it was the problem. We ventured out — got lost. I kept a slip of paper with the address of the hotel written on it. Whenever we couldn't find our way we hailed a taxi, showed the driver the paper, and in a few minutes were back at the hotel, ready to try again. The driver charged me anywhere from ten cruzeiros to fifty, depending on how bewildered I looked — it seemed. But we saw Rio — Copacabana Beach, Sugar Loaf Mountain, Corcovado, and all. We learned how to ask directions, the price of things, the value of cruzeiros, and how to like coal-black coffee swimming with sugar. We were seasoned travelers in Brazil. Now for Sao Paulo!

"Upon arriving at the airport in Sao Paulo we were greeted by an ocean of Japanese faces. They all looked alike to us. Surely Sao Paulo must be a Japanese city! In all that group, could we find some one that we knew or who knew us? Much to our surprise, we found that they had *all* come to greet us. These foreigners from America, the long-looked-for missionaries had arrived. We, believe it or not, were the center of attention. Welcoming meetings, fiestas, Japanese dinners, and tours through the city were the order of the days ahead.

" 'What, no car?' I asked in amazement. I was surprised that all the world didn't own cars as in the United States. 'No, we must travel by *bonde*', they said. '*Bonde?* Where did streetcars get such a name?' They told me all about it. But how to get on one? They were full, completely packed. And yet, scores of people were still climbing on the running board which extended along the full length of the open car. We tried it, too, but they squeezed us off. We would ride the *onibus*. But those lines of people, a block long! Those were the days when the streetcar fare was only twenty centavos, and the bus fare was fifty. Even though we had to wait for the bus, at least we could get inside and not be squeezed off.

"Someone wisely informed us that there were just two classes of pedestrians in Sao Paulo, the 'quick' and the 'dead.' After jumping and dodging traffic for several days, I concluded that if ever I had a car down here, I wouldn't care much if it had brakes or not, but one thing I must sure to have — a dandy, good blasting horn in excellent working order to scare the daylights out of anyone who dared get in my way!

"Sao Paulo seemed to be the liveliest, most optimistic and aggressive city I had ever seen! Prices were high. There was work for everyone. Real estate was booming. Building construction was contagious. Farmers were selling their land, moving into the city to invest in get-rich-quick schemes. In the few days that we were in Sao Paulo, we were taken to many places and shown many properties. True, our Mission would want to buy, but we were not prepared for the high prices.

"But were we sent to Brazil? No, they said it was Paraguay.

" 'Paraguay?' our church brethren asked. 'Why do you

want to go there? Nothing there. Backward.'

" 'But we were appointed. We must be on our way.'

"So, one day we bid farewell to Brazil and our friends there and took to the air."

Chapter 4

Providential Delay

Soon after the appointment of Helen Voller and me to Brazil, I began to correspond with the Reverend Daniel Nishizumi. On December 14, 1945, he wrote:

"... with very happy [sic] I received your fine letter today. We are very glad you and others come to work with us for the Lord. We thank the Lord that opened the way for our mission to Brazil. We welcome you."

On January 28, 1946, he said:

"... we are praying for you to come as soon as possible, and also for Bishop Ormston and Rev. Byron Lamson. It is very necessary to work for the Lord in Brazil. We sent a letter regarding the climate and other things in the city of Sao Paulo. But in the country it is very different. The climate is very warm and the civilization is very behind, the schools are very few and many people without education. First, we need our seminary and church and mission school in Sao Paulo city and after we must extend to every place. We need very much a leader. Please pray for us and the work of the Lord."

In early March, Bishop Ormston and the missionary secretary made a trip to Brazil and Paraguay to prepare the way for the missionaries. Following the instructions of the missionary board, they purchased the Good Samaritan Orphanage property in Asunción. Thanks to the Sunday schools, there was on hand almost fifty thousand dollars for purchase of property and the equipping and sending of missionaries.

While Bishop Ormston and Dr. Lamson were in Brazil they met with the Japanese pastors and worked out a plan for financial aid to be given them so they could give full time to the ministry. All the pastors then had secular employment. Also, arrangements were made with the Reverend and Mrs. José Emerenciano, personal friends of Mr. Nishizumi, to work with the new missionaries among the Brazilians. Mr. Emerenciano, a true Brazilian from the northeast, had a good knowledge of English and Japanese and a wide acquaintance in evangelical circles in many parts of Brazil.

When Helen Voller and I arrived in Santos, Daniel Nishizumi met us, helped us through customs, and took us on the bus up the mountain (twenty-five hundred feet) to the wide plateau where Sao Paulo is located. At that time, Sao Paulo was a city of about one and a half million and was called the fastest growing city in the world. (Today it is a teeming megalopolis of skyscrapers and industries with a population of more than ten million.) How glad we were that the Ryckmans were still in Sao Paulo and were at the same hotel where Nishizumi took us — The Palace, on Florencio de Abreu Street in the heart of the city. It was a small, inexpensive hotel where the price included room and meals. It was June — winter in Brazil — a dreary and cold day with no heat in the rooms. It all added up to a feeling of loneliness in this strange land of Portuguese-speaking people. But all of that would change within a few months to a real love for people and country.

During those days, as Brother Nishizumi took us and the Ryckmans to look at different properties, we began to feel acquainted with this gentle and kind Christlike man. He was concerned about *us* as well as the Mission and was trying to locate a small living accommodation for Helen and me.

Then the day came for Harold, Evalyn, and Don to leave for Paraguay. In typical Brazilian and Japanese fashion, a big group was at the airport to say good-bye.

When Harold presented their tickets at the counter, the attendant said: "You will not be going to Asunción this morning. That plane has already left!"

In disbelief Harold replied: "But look at the time written on these tickets!"

"Sorry, but that plane leaves at 8:00 A.M. — not 9:00."

They found it would be one month before they could get three reservations again.

A few mornings later, our hotel phone rang and I heard Dr. Hayashi's voice saying, "Miss Damon, Brother Nishizumi was in an accident this morning. He was hit by a truck while crossing the street after he got off a bus. He is in the Hospital das Clinicas."

What shocking news! How thankful Helen and I were that in God's providence the Ryckmans were still in Sao Paulo. We went to the hospital but were unable to see our brother. That night before his spirit was released from his broken body, Nishizumi said to his brother-in-law, "My work is finished. Meet me in heaven."

At the memorial service, someone kindly wrote for us, in English, a brief summary of each tribute, which I have kept. As I look over these papers I find repeated again and again the words "goodness" and "humility." Dr. Kinoshita, a lawyer, said, "Daniel Nishizumi's life was a great inspiration to me. I feel that I must now live, serve, and pray for Christ's kingdom to come here to Brazil." And Dr. Kinoshita has done just that. He was one of the first delegates from Brazil to our General Conference in Winona Lake in 1964. In addition, he has given invaluable legal service to the mission and church.

The leader of the Japanese Free Methodist Church in Brazil was gone! "What now?" all of us were asking. At that point, God used His servant, Harold Ryckman, in a remarkable way. With his years of experience as pastor and superintendent, he knew how to proceed. It was evident that the people had great confidence in him. Calling the pastors and laymen together, Harold asked them to choose one from their group to assume leadership. They agreed on the Reverend Seiti Simizu, who was then employed as an accountant out in the interior of the state of Sao Paulo. They contacted him and asked that he get released as soon as possible to give full time to the church.

During those decision-making days, José Emerenciano gave invaluable help with his knowledge of both English and Japanese. Steps were also taken regarding his move to Sao Paulo.

A day or two after these meetings, Harold said to Evalyn, "I think I have done all I can to help the church here. What will we do while we are waiting for our flight to Asunción?"

Scarcely had he finished, when a phone call came from the airline. A voice said, "We have cancellations for three people on the flight tomorrow for Paraguay. Do you want them?"

Once more we all went to the airport for a farewell. After the plane lifted, Helen and I really did feel alone in that big city.

I have heard Harold recount what happened after they left:

"When we were settled on the plane, I said to Evalyn, 'How are we going to find the Good Samaritan Orphanage? That telegram we sent the Hendricksons yesterday will never reach them this soon. Without doubt, the airport is out in the middle of nowhere. Furthermore, we don't even have a street address of our destination!'

"Evalyn merely said, 'Honey, if the Lord has taken care of us thus far, don't you think He is able for this also?'

"When the plane landed, it was just as I had said — out in a big field. We were the last ones to descend. At once, an American I had never met stepped up and said,

'Are you Harold Ryckman?' In utter amazement I answered, 'Yes.' He continued, 'I'm Ray Mills. I have a taxi waiting to take you to the orphanage.'

" 'But how did you know we were coming?' I questioned. Ray Mills was a missionary of another denomination with whom I had corresponded once or twice previously.

"His reply was, "I was downtown in Asunción this morning, and if ever the Holy Spirit spoke to me, it was then. He told me to get a taxi and get right out to the airport because Harold Ryckman was coming in!' "

They were taken right to the gate of the property where they would live and work for the major part of the next five years. The Hendricksons, though taken by surprise, gave them a warm welcome.

After a little more than a week's orientation, the Ryckmans were left on their own in charge of the orphanage with its twenty-one girls, including helpers and teachers. One or two of the latter had a fair knowledge of English and thus could interpret. It was difficult, though, to have so much responsibility so soon.

The mission property consisted of five acres of land about four miles from the center of Asunción. It had once been the home of a retired English sea captain. For many years it had been the Instituto Samaritano, also known as Quinta las Violctas, operated by independent missionaries, the Reverend and Mrs. Ford Hendrickson.

Harold Ryckman, twelve years old, in Chino, California

Evalyn, Donald, and Harold Ryckman, 1951

Harold, Evalyn, and Donald, packing up for Brazil in 1946

Church and Bible School buildings, Paraguay

Skyscrapers, water, and mountains make Rio de Janeiro a
beauty spot.

Rock formations as viewed from Rio de Janeiro

First Free Methodist Church in Sao Paulo, November 7, 1963;
Daniel Nishizumi, standing at right

Ordination of pastors by Superintendent Harold Ryckman and
Area Secretary E. C. Snyder. Candidates (l. to r.): Taisuke
Sakuma, Sukeiti Ono, and Kinzo Uchida

Harold and Evalyn Ryckman, Brazil, 1955

First portable tabernacle in Campos do Jordao (l. to r.): Wesley
Hankins, Harold Ryckman, Donald Bowen

Wesley Hankins giving diploma at Asunción Bible School

First headquarters building in Sao Paulo

Seminary building in Sao Paulo

45

Brazil seminary, first residence completed

Brazil seminary. Dean Mizuki and President Bowen presenting diplomas to graduates of Christian education course, 1959

One of the professor's homes in Spring Arbor of Brazil

Girls' dormitory at the seminary

Chapter 5

New Adjustments

When a rookie missionary begins his new life in a foreign field there are many adjustments which he must make or he will not make it. One reason mission boards send out young people still in their twenties is that they usually can adjust more easily to a change of life-style. For our new South American work, our Board deliberately chose people of more years as the pioneers. They felt they would need a backlog of experience.

Some of Harold's early frustrations show up in his September, 1946, letter to the Board. Though he was the writer, the letter was signed also by Evalyn Ryckman, Esther Harris, and Ruth Foy. Excerpts follow:

"This letter represents our first formal yearly report to the General Board from our new work in Paraguay. While mission work is new to all of us here, and since this is a new field, we trust that you will make allowances for our poor methods or lack of judgment or misunderstanding of the missionary system. I shall try to give a picture of the field and work as frankly as I am able.

"The Ryckman family arrived in Paraguay about two and a half months ago. Misses Harris and Foy arrived here about a month later. We have all found plenty to keep us busy and are, little by little, getting our work organized so that each carries a portion of the responsibilities. While the radical change of climate, food, and customs has affected all of us somewhat, we are reasonably happy, blessed, and physically well.

"These are naturally trying days, making adjustments socially, overcoming language handicaps, etc. Our greatest trial is in our not being able to be more aggressive in evangelistic lines. We see so much to be done, but since we have by no means mastered the language nor learned the Latin psychology, we must content ourselves by making promises for the future. We are now holding four services each week for the girls of the Home. Each missionary takes part.... A week ago Sunday night, after I had spoken about their finding their place in life and filling it, there was a real melting time when in a voluntary way about a dozen of them began seeking the Lord for forgiveness...."

There followed a detailed description of the condition of the property and the needs for various improvements. Then the letter continued in regard to the purpose of the orphanage:

"We are convinced that a real need is being met in the giving of a Home and training to these girls. But there are some very real problems.... What is to be the *objective?* When these girls become of age and are ready to leave, what then? ... The normal thing is for them to look forward to marriage and a home.... Where can we find clean Christian companions for them? ... They have no outside contacts. Their being secluded here all their lives is a most abnormal situation. When released from this Home and turned into the world, they naturally become an easy mark for the very thing we are trying to avoid. What should we do to combat this? ... We are giving ourselves to a study of the problem....

"We are continuing to look for the proper location for a church.... It might not be bad to build right here in such a location that we could invite the neighbors in to the services.... Pray for us.... There is a *field of evangelism and this is, of course, our prime objective in being here."*

*   *   *

From the beginning, Harold found much of his daylight time filled with repairing and keeping up the property. Without a car, his frequent trips to the city involved walking part way on the dusty road, then taking a crowded bus with ceiling so low he could not stand up straight, and finally transferring to a streetcar.

On certain days the missionaries had a class in Spanish with a teacher. Most of Harold's personal study had to be done at night. At first, it was by the light of a gasoline pressure lamp. Then gasoline became unavailable and it was by carbide, wax, or tallow candlelight. Finally, even the latter could not be bought, and a lighted wick in oil became the substitute. Night study was always accompanied by the zooming hordes of mosquitoes in the room. A net gave some relief during the sleeping hours.

Don was having his adjustments, too. He attended the Colegio International in Asunción, a mission school with all classes in Spanish. Before long he was speaking Spanish easily and was also picking up the Guarani (the indigenous language). He had a gift in languages as well as in music. In addition to piano lessons, he learned to play the guitar and the Paraguayan harp.

Es Muy Lindo

When missionaries first arrive in a country, they are impressed by what seems new and different — scenery, climate, food, customs. After a time, all becomes so familiar they no longer "see" as they did at first. The following chapter presents some of Harold's early impressions of Paraguay. It is taken from a letter which appeared in the January 1947 *Missionary Tidings*.

"Here in Paraguay we have an expression which is used to describe almost every condition which is over on the sunny side of the ledger of life — *es muy lindo* — 'It is very beautiful.' It seems to fit when describing the beauties of nature, when pleased with the weather, when expressing the delicate taste of a choice morsel of food, or perhaps the congenial disposition of a friend. The countenances of these people shine with an approving smile when this expression is used concerning their homeland.

"From the gay musical notes of colorful, flitting birds, the majestic splendor of these stately royal palms, the delightful fragrance and beauty of the wild orange trees, the lush profusion of semitropical plants midst romantic beauty under southern skies, from stately homes, the tiled rooftops and shining tile floors so beautifully patterned come one prevailing sentiment — es muy lindo.

"But all is not as *muy lindo* as one might be led to believe by glancing at surface conditions. Autocratic oppression and devastating wars have, through the centuries, transformed this country, once the capital of

South America, into a land of instability and unprogres-
siveness. (In 1860, the population of Paraguay was more
than one million. But in 1865, Paraguay engaged in a war
against Argentina, Uruguay, and Brazil. When the war
ended in 1870, upon the death of the Paraguayan leader,
the population had been reduced to about two hundred
fifty thousand, of which only fifty thousand were men!) A
disrupting spirit of unrest and revenge, fomenting distrust
and revolt, surges everywhere. Unequal distribution of
wealth and opportunity, religious intolerance, poverty,
and ignorance are on every hand. A few of the more
educated are struggling to bring more modern methods,
conveniences, and progressive ideals. But it is a tedious
process.

"The biblical picture of the rich man faring sumptu-
ously every day while Lazarus, swathed in rags and with
festering sores, waits hungrily at the gate is literally a
common picture in Paraguay. To the gate of our
orphanage, Quinta las Violetas, come nearly every day
those whose needs — physically, materially, and most of
all, spiritually — are greater than we can describe. May
God grant us wisdom that we may know how to give,
wisely, such help as Christ would give, were He here.

"A few days past I attended a funeral. It was one of
the better class families whose mother had died. The
crowd was large. Elaboration abounded. Ceremonies were
profuse. From the church there was a funeral march
through the cemetery to the burial vault on the far side.
This was all in order, but my heart was touched to see the
many who stepped aside from the procession to fall
prostrate upon the grave of one of their loved ones as with
heart-piercing shrieks and wails they poured out from
their hearts their deep trouble concerning eternal things
and the hopelessness and despair pent up within. What
assurance Christ would bring to these hearts if they were
brought to a true knowledge of His saving power!

"Hundreds of people pass by on the road in front of us

each day. Surrounding us are hundreds of homes, varying from the mansions of the very rich to the tiny *casitas* ('little mud houses') of *los pobres*. From the center of Asunción, four miles to the south, to Trinidad, two miles north, there is no other evangelical group working. We have talked to some of our neighbors and find them hungry for the gospel. Daily, we give tracts and gospels to all who come to our gate. Our hearts burn to be able to talk to them more freely and to start religious services soon. But the limitation of the language is ours yet. Conversationally we get by in the stores, in the Home, on the bus, and with the neighbors. But we need to learn both Spanish and Guarani. This is our task for the present.

"In the meantime, we have a family of twenty-one girls whom we are trying to train in Christian living. We have four religious services each week for them....

"There are many more things we could tell you of this country *muy lindo*. But we shall save them for another time ... and just add a few suggestions for definite prayer. Some of these needs are very practical and urgent and necessary for our best health and advancement. Please pray for:

1. Our car to arrive soon.
2. Electricity to be connected soon.
3. Water pressure system and sanitary equipment.
4. Salvation of all the girls in the Home.
5. Leading concerning the opening of a Bible school, a clinic, and a vocational school.
6. The building of a nice chapel on or near this property.

"Yes, truly this is a beautiful country, and we thank God every day for the beauty in the foreground of the picture, for it helps to distract one's attention from the dark ugliness in the background — the ugliness of sin.

"It is spring down here, and our hearts and hopes are high with the vision of great possibilities for the spreading of God's work in the heart of the land of the Southern Cross.

"Keep the prayers going up and the letters coming south and know that we appreciate so much all you have done and are doing for us."

"Yours sincerely,
"Harold and Evalyn."

Chapter 7

Family Crisis

Inexperienced missionaries on new fields, without the support of an established organization or the counsel of senior colleagues, face almost insurmountable obstacles. This is especially true in providing even basic living arrangements, sanitation, and health safeguards.

Letters from the pioneering Ryckmans tell the story:

"Asunción
"June 2, 1947

"Dear Friends of Ours:

"Can it be possible that a whole year has slipped by since we sailed into the harbor at Rio de Janeiro? Yet in some ways it seems years ago, so much has happened since then. We are the same Harold, Evalyn, and Donald you knew in the U.S. — and yet we aren't. But we still love you all and miss you much. We still covet your prayers and your letters. We still love our Lord and are happy to serve Him wherever He leads. We still have a burden for the lost around us and for those near you.

"I have been rereading some of your letters lately and the questions repeat themselves: How are you *really?* What are you doing? What do you need? What are your aims? I shall try to answer some of them.

"The weather is perfect these winter days, though we nearly froze a week ago. Remember, in Paraguay there is no heat in houses. Yes, we have had considerable illness this last year, due to changes in weather, diet, unsanitary conditions, poor transportation, and overwork. We nearly lost Don two weeks ago (spinal meningitis); yesterday he climbed to the top of a tall tree! Today he walked over three miles. Wednesday he will go back to school with no complications or aftereffects. All praise be to our Heavenly Father!

"The revolution still drags on. . . . Prices are exorbitant, food is scarce, building materials are impossible. Gasoline, kerosine, sugar, and other things are rationed. But we are safe under God's protection, so do not worry about us. Keep praying.

"We speak Spanish most of the time now, and often write it. But we make no brags as to how well. For two months, Harold has had a young men's Bible class and Evalyn a children's Bible story hour each week, in Spanish, of course. The other missionaries and some of the girls of the Home have just started a ten- or fifteen-minute service just inside the gate for those who come at stated times to receive used clothing. We have given out thousands of tracts, gospels, and Testaments since we came — not just promiscuously, but to definite contacts.

"Harold, with unskilled national help, has installed septic tanks, a toilet in our house, built the garage and workshop, put in more windows in the girls' sleeping rooms, installed shelves and cupboards, cleaned and rebuilt the well. He is putting in fifty orange trees, has lots of garden planted, has taken care of the general upkeep and repairs which are many around this type of institution. This in addition to being daddy and pastor to the orphanage and holding regular services. Evalyn has looked after the general health of everybody (except herself) and done nearly a thousand treatments, dressings, etc. Without a car, her numerous treks taking children to the Health Center in the city have been very taxing on her strength. . . .

"Our aims and aspirations? Probably most of all we

need a chapel, a place to hold services for the people around us. There is no other evangelical work within miles. We will start a Sunday school for the outsiders in a month or so in the new garage. We will soon outgrow it. Evalyn needs clinic rooms and another nurse. We want to have a Bible school. Then, after the work in this needy, neglected section is established, we would like to turn it over to a young couple so Harold can go out into evangelistic work elsewhere, probably nearer the city. So pray and pray and give to missions.

"Write often. With much love,

"Yours in His service,
"Harold and Evalyn."

The *Missionary Tidings* (August 1948) gives an inside account of the war and fighting near the campus. Harold also gives other details regarding the serious illness of his son, Don. He writes:

"We have just experienced a revolution. Result? The party in power is still here. Forty thousand men left the country and many of them will never return. While our mission has been here only a little more than a year, we were able to be of some help during this upheaval.

"When the fighting was near and cannon and machine gun fire were flying over our property, many refugees, women and children, came to our place for protection. At times, more than one hundred found asylum here. Some brought their little crude altars. With candles burning, they knelt and prayed. Others in groups chanted memorized prayers, while still others sat apart.

"What were we to do? Our use of the Spanish language was so limited and many of them understood only Guarani, of which we knew nothing. But we must do something to help them. So, asking God's help, we entered in, singing gospel hymns, reading portions of God's word, praying, and teaching them of the love of Jesus.

"The next night even more people came, but there

were no altars nor candles.... Anxiously they were waiting for the service to begin. Thus it continued for more than a week. Their interest and appreciation seemed exceedingly great.

"Then the danger passed and they stayed in their homes. The immediate result seemed small. There was no great awakening, it seemed. Yet it was a challenge to launch out with the gospel message."

Don's siege with spinal meningitis was a severe family crisis. One day Don came home from school saying, "Mom, I have the worst headache I have ever had!" Medical consultation revealed spinal meningitis. The doctor decided that Don could have better care right at home with his own mother as his nurse.

"Don steadily grew worse. When the Paraguayan doctor came late one afternoon he shook his head after his examination. Don's back was curved and he was breathing in chain strokes, all indicative of approaching death.

"Evalyn and I decided to take turns with the 'watch.' She agreed to take the early part of the night and I the latter. I went to my study to pray. I told the Lord all about it once more. Then I began to read the ninety-first Psalm. As I meditated on it verse by verse, it seemed to be talking to *me* in the use of thou and thy. 'But what about my son?' I asked of the Lord. Then as I read on to the fourteenth verse, I saw that the pronoun changed to the third person. 'Because he hath set his love upon me, therefore will I deliver him: ... With long life will I satisfy him, and show him my salvation.'

"God gave me a quiet peace in my heart, and I went to sleep with the expectation of getting up in the middle of the night. But when I awoke, the sun was streaming in the windows. I jumped up, ran to the bedroom and found both Don and Evalyn sleeping. She soon awoke and said, 'Why, what has happened? Things are different in here.'

"At that moment, Don sat up in bed and said, 'Mom, I'm hungry!' What a change!

"Before long the doctor came and was amazed at what he saw. He asked Don to get out of bed and walk a few steps. 'Remarkable!' was his comment. 'There is no trace of the disease and no aftereffects. I can't believe it! I told my wife last night that I never again expected to see Don alive.'

" 'Doctor,' " I said. " 'We prayed and God answered.' "

Chapter 8

Does It Pay?

After two years of hard work, some illness, and many frustrations, the missionaries began to see visible results in lives being changed by Christ. Harold wrote to his friends and prayer partners:

"We are encouraged for the work both here and in Brazil. Our Sunday school is growing. Last Sunday seventy people almost pushed out the garage walls. A new mothers' class, doubled attendance at YPMS and JMS meetings, and twenty-three young men in our home last night for the Bible class are all encouraging signs of the last few months.

"The new chapel is started, the well is drilled, and the windmill is being erected. We have put a kitchen and a bath in our house and done much remodeling and painting of the orphanage property. Daily, Evalyn treats sick people, mostly children and babies, giving medicines and used clothing in our front hall which serves as her clinic room."

The Reverend Orlando Palella, an Argentinian, and his Paraguayan wife came to work with the mission that year. Hopes were high that they would be used of the Lord in the expansion of the work. In 1950, Miss Elizabeth Reynolds, R.N., was appointed to Paraguay.

The chapel was ready for use in 1949. Harold had designed and engineered the project, which turned out to be a beautiful set of buildings. He surveyed the completed work with a great sense of satisfaction — a dream become reality. Best of all, several of the Paraguayan men who had worked with him on the job had opened their hearts to the Lord Jesus.

In early February, 1950, about two hundred fifty people attended the dedication service. Representatives of the Baptists, Disciples, Brethren, New Testament Mission, and the YMCA shared in the service. It was a significant event. Harold said:

"What a holy joy thrills our hearts as we realize that the glorious message of the saving and sanctifying grace of our Lord Jesus Christ is going forth in South America to those who have been living in superstition and ignorance of God's love and true plan for their lives."

South of the equator, spring comes in September, Christmas in the midst of summer, and Easter in autumn. The summer heat varies, of course, according to the latitude, altitude, and distance from the ocean. Paraguay does become very hot. All his life, Harold had found heat oppressive. As a youth working in the hay fields of Chino and as a pastor in Phoenix, he had frequently endured temperatures of one hundred fifteen to one hundred twenty degrees. His letter of November gives his reaction to the heat; but more important, his answer to a penetrating question:

"Asunción,
"November 25, 1950
"Dear Friends in the Homeland:
"This is a hot, humid, and sultry forenoon. Perspiration drips, and the sun burns down with a penetrating heat that seems to go clear through one. This is Paraguayan summer. But it isn't always this way. Agreeable changes come with a heavy rain and southern breezes.

"Often since coming here I have asked myself, 'Has it paid to follow the Lord, leave all and come out to this country that I knew nothing about and enter into missionary service?' Four years out here prove that it is always safest to follow Him. His way is best.

"Life here has not always been easy. There have been difficulties, oppositions, misunderstandings, and deceptions surrounding us continually. Sometimes the problems mount until it seems there is no way through. But the way *up* has never once been closed. Our Christ has never failed us. He is leading on to victory. When He comes in, the problems melt away. Yes, it has paid. . . . But payday hasn't come yet. This is but the sowing time — harvest comes in due season.

"While my responsibilities now cover the work both here and in Brazil, most of my time has been spent in Paraguay. . . . We had thought of moving to Brazil where the larger part of our work is located, but so far have been unable to do so. This has required frequent trips over there. . . .

"Our work here in Paraguay, outside of merely maintaining a small orphanage for girls, began in earnest less than three years ago. During this time we have introduced and maintained a Sunday school, preaching services, Bible classes, and youth activities for the people of the community. A great deal of favorable interest, as well as fanatical opposition, has been aroused. Our Sunday school varies but maintains an average of close to one hundred. The Sunday evening preaching service attendance runs around sixty-five. The young people's group has about thirty-five. We have had many conversions. Some of the people vacillate in their fidelity. Recently we have had the joy of baptizing twenty of the faithful ones after many months of indoctrinating and proving them. Although we are seeing an awakening in spiritual things among the girls of the orphanage, there are only a few of them ready for baptism."

"Sincerely, your friends,
"Harold and Evalyn."

The prison experience described in the Introduction of

this book took place the same month this letter was written. In January, Harold came to Sao Paulo to preside at the conference. We observed in him an afterglow of the persecution he had suffered for Jesus' sake.

Furlough came for the Ryckmans in June of 1951, in time to attend the General Conference. When they arrived at the New York airport, Harold gave their luggage to a porter and walked along talking to him in Spanish. Why didn't the man understand? Finally, he realized where he was!

Chapter 9

I Saw Iguassu

Among Harold's papers is a delightful description of his first view of the famous Iguassu Falls, lying partly in Brazil and partly in Argentina. He wrote from Asunción in 1947:

"When a Christian dedicates his life to God and His work, he many times thinks only of the sacrifices and hardships which he must endure. He thinks of the cross, of crucifixion, and of self-denial. Especially is this true of the missionary. He goes out not knowing whither he goes. He expects to burn out his life, and willingly, in loving service for the brethren. And it is well that he should think this way. All is not easy, neither is everything pleasant.

"But there is another side, a refreshing aspect which is not presented to us in the beginning. There are times of surprising joy which come to us unexpectedly, right in the midst of the most trying circumstances. I speak of experiences of inspiration and beauty, one of which I was permitted to enjoy on one of my trips to Brazil. Problems had been heavy. I was weary both in body and spirit. I was making my way from one set of difficulties to enter into the midst of others. But our Heavenly Father knew just what was needed to quicken my spirit and refresh my mind. He opened the clouds and let the healing rays of nature's beauty flood my soul for a few minutes. It was such a tonic to my being that I am sure I shall never forget it.

"The pilot of the plane, a Douglas DC-3, of the *Pamair do Brasil* line, had told me that if the sky was clear when we were ready to leave the airport at Iguassu, he would swing out over the falls. Much to my joy, it was clear; and just as we were boarding the plane, he whispered in my ear, 'In a few minutes we will be over the falls.'

"A pause at the end of the runway, a brief testing of the motors and the controls, a mighty lunge, and the craft was speeding down the grassy field. In another moment the tail lifted and we were literally flying over the ground. Just when it happened, I could never determine; but suddenly we were looking down on the tops of palms and jungle flora. Just across the river from Paraguay, we passed over the little border town of Iguassu in Brazil. To the right flowed the mighty Parana River. Fifteen miles straight ahead we could see the steaming curtain of vapor which ascends from the angry, churning waters of Iguassu Falls.

"In a bare five minutes the pilot flung open the door separating the cockpit from the passengers, and said, 'Look on the left!' That was my side. For a minute all was hidden beneath the wing of the plane. But above and ahead could be seen the mists of the falls. Then suddenly the plane tilted sharply to the left, the wing lowered and behold, Iguassu! At that time of the year, the rainy season, it is the largest waterfall in the world. I wanted a photograph, but the use of cameras was forbidden.

"There has been some dispute as to which is the greatest: Victoria, Niagara, or Iguassu. Of course, we here in South America claim Iguassu. Its width is approximately two and a half miles — more than the crest of both Niagara and Victoria combined. The height is two hundred feet. Niagara boasts only one hundred sixty-seven, but Victoria is four hundred. The volume of water flowing over Niagara is more constant and is greater most of the time. But during the rainy season, now at its height, the Iguassu flow is double that of Niagara.

Victoria equals Iguassu most of the year.

"But, as for sheer, enchanting beauty, Iguassu has no rival. The natural beauty of this wild jungle setting, unspoiled as yet by modern progress, enhances the charm of the scene. The Iguassu River above, marking for many miles the border between Argentina and Brazil, wending its crooked way quietly and serenely through the dense forests, comes abruptly to the edge of a high plateau. There is no exciting rush of rapids to the crest of the falls. Rather, it seems to hesitate and spread itself into a broad fan, waiting politely until all is in readiness for a united plunge of the whole river in one great climax of scenic splendor just before it loses its identity in the great Parana. Iguassu is broken up into many hundreds of waterspouts which plunge over the brink between jungle-covered islands. The main portion is in the form of a great horseshoe, pouring its waters from three sides into a churning, foaming gorge, called *Garganta do Diabo* (the devil's throat), which angrily spews its water out into the river below. After about eight miles of churning and boiling, it empties itself into the Parana.

"The plane, dangerously low, made a complete circle around the falls. We saw it from a great vantage point. But it was so brief — a few minutes of entrancing splendor as we cut through the mists of the smoking water. From every angle we beheld its gigantic beauty refracted through ever-changing rainbow hues. Then, suddenly the plane righted itself, straightened out and went its way onward above the trackless forest jungles of Brazil. The falls were behind, but the vision remained. I became aware that I had had the rare privilege of seeing one of God's natural wonders of the world. But an urge was pressing my soul. I must go back some day and stand there on the ground and gaze at this angry glory where flowering jungles crowd its bank, bright-plumed birds sing their shrill songs, and wild animals come down to the river to drink."

69

And he did have that privilege several times and took pictures to his heart's content. In 1971 we shared that joy together as we returned to Brazil after Harold had held the annual conference in Asunción. We spent two wonderful days at the falls.

Chapter 10

"Come Over and Help Us"

After the Ryckmans had gone on to Paraguay in 1946, Helen and I moved into a small, two-room apartment in the Vila Mariana district of Sao Paulo. Our rent was fifty dollars a month, which seemed very high for those times. The Emerencianos also moved from Barretos into a rented house in Vila Mariana. All of us working together began a Sunday school and worship service in their living room. This was the beginning of a new Brazilian church.

We continued to search for suitable property for a church and mission residence. In October we found two lots on a strategic corner in a new area, called Mirandopolis. It was near the Emerenciano house. On a Saturday afternoon Mr. Emerenciano, Dr. Hayashi, Sr., Onoda, Helen, and I stood on that empty land, our heads bowed, while one of the men prayed that God would enable us to buy it if it was His will. In my own heart I believed the Holy Spirit whispered, "This is the place."

The missionary secretary asked Harold to go to Sao Paulo to give his counsel. After a careful survey, he judged the corner lots to be the best. Price of land was so high that the Board directed the purchase of only one lot. This was done.

However, our hearts were heavy because of lack of space for future expansion. We began to meet weekly with a little group to pray about the matter. God answered. The Board agreed to provide a certain amount for the second lot if we could raise a specified quantity in Brazil.

71

Although the new property would be for the Brazilian church, our Japanese people contributed liberally. By June of 1947 the transaction was complete.

A plan developed for the Ryckman family to come to Sao Paulo for a few months of vacation, as they called it, so that Harold could take charge of the construction. Shortly after Thanksgiving, digging began for the two-story building. A chapel was to occupy the first floor and a five-room living apartment, the second.

When the Japanese pastors and laymen had their customary annual meeting in January, Harold was asked to preside at the business session. The group voted to write the Missionary Board to request the transfer of the Ryckmans to Brazil.

Dr. Lamson wrote Harold for his reaction. His reply:

"Ever since we first landed here in June of 1946, even before the death of Brother Nishizumi, these people seemed to be convinced that we should remain in Brazil. . . . But, of course, we were scheduled for Paraguay.

"Personally, I have from the beginning felt as if Brazil was my place. Yes, I must confess that I do have an urge in this direction — not because of healthier living conditions, though they are better, but because there seems to be a mutual understanding between my heart and the heart of these people. I also seem to have a vision for the work here."

In June, the Commission on Missions requested Harold to serve as superintendent for South America "in order to unify the work." Their thought was for him to divide his time between Paraguay and Brazil. Their letter closed with, "We trust that you will accept this appointment as from the church and in the will of the Lord. We wish you every success and assure you of our complete confidence and full cooperation."

Replying on July 30, 1948, Harold wrote:

"I will try to do the best I can in promoting the work in both fields. There are many dreams and plans, but it will take time and a lot of work to begin even to realize them."

The Ryckmans had to return to Paraguay in June before the construction was fully completed. But Harold came to Sao Paulo for the dedication of the new building in September. After that, Helen and I moved into the apartment above the chapel. Just before the dedication, the new missionaries, James and Mary Grier Junker arrived. They soon moved to Campinas, a beautiful city of about one hundred thousand population, just two hours by bus from Sao Paulo. There they studied Portuguese in the new language school for missionaries.

Growth of the Japanese churches was remarkable. Mr. Simizu was now in Sao Paulo as superintendent and pastor of the church which met in his house. Their Sunday school was increasing phenomenally. In getting their first daily vacation Bible school organized, Miss Voller gave them invaluable help. Dr. Hayashi owned and operated a dental laboratory, but on Sundays he preached in one place or another and on week nights had a meeting in various homes.

Harold's report to Dr. Lamson describes the Brazil success story:

"I wish I could describe to you in words the healthy condition of this work among the Japanese. These people are really on fire for God, yet far from being fanatical. They carry on aggressively and sacrifice greatly for the work. They have several fine new works started in the interior in the heart of large Japanese settlements. . . . There are more than a half million Japanese in the state of Sao Paulo alone. . . . They have broken away from Japan and the old religions . . . are wide open for the Gospel of Jesus Christ. . . . There are only two other groups that are giving special attention to the Japanese colony.''

In our appropriation requests we asked for a big increase in funds for evangelism. To support this petition, Harold wrote:

''It seems to me that we spend a lot of money on the 'means' and neglect the 'end.' The spearpoint of all of our work is getting the message to the people. Missionaries' salaries, language study, rent, pastors' salaries, educational costs, permanent improvements — all are for the purpose of doing just one thing. . . . If we have our hands tied because of lack of finances for evangelism, we defeat our purpose.

''This Japanese harvest is ripe. The doors are open and we must move in at once. Our workers are ready and eager. But we are limited by lack of money for transportation, literature, money to rent halls, food for workers on trips, etc.

''I made a trip with one of our young Japanese pastors last weekend to Marilia . . . about four hundred miles from here. We want to send Brother Sakuma there next year as soon as he finishes at the Methodist seminary. I am sure we shall see a great harvest in Marilia. The cost of this one trip for the two of us was about forty dollars, but it was abundantly worthwhile. Our money spent for evangelism is paying the greatest dividends of any. . . . It is the spearpoint of all our other efforts. . . . Let's keep it sharp! I have great hopes for Brazil!''

In the book, *The Growth of Japanese Churches in Brazil* (William Carey Library, 533 Hermosa Street, South Pasadena, CA 91030, © 1978 by John Mizuki), there is one chapter on the Free Methodist Church. The author, Dr. John Mizuki, summarizes the reasons for the rapid growth from 1948-59 during which the Free Methodist Church went from 136 members to 1,091. He states that one important factor was ''the aid, financial and in missionary personnel, given by the Missionary Board. The financial aid enabled the national workers to give full time to church planting. Shimizu ... returned to a full-time ministry in 1947. Three seminarians, Kinzo Uchida, Taisuke Sakuma, and John Mizuki, who graduated respectively in 1947, 1948, 1949, went directly into full-time" (page 82).

Another factor Mizuki presents was the revival that began in 1947. He describes the coming of the Holy Spirit upon the people in a Sunday morning service at an annual retreat in Santo Amaro. The Reverend Juro Yuasa of the Holiness Church was the speaker. While he was preaching, the hearers began to weep quietly. Mizuki says, "The revival lifted up the spiritual condition of the Free Methodist people who enjoyed a wonderful spiritual unity which contributed for the growth of the Church in the following years" (page 83).

Chapter 11

Spring Arbor in Brazil

One of Daniel Nishizumi's dreams was for a Free Methodist seminary in Brazil. When we arrived in Sao Paulo, the three ministerial candidates were in other denominational schools. Bishop Ormston and Dr. Lamson had returned from Sao Paulo in early 1946 with a strong impression of this need for a seminary. So, that had been in our planning," wrote Harold.

Harold's vision was for both evangelism and education as indicated by a statement in a letter of 1950:

"It is not a question of whether it will be evangelism *or* education. It will be both and they will work hard hand in hand."

When Harold and Evalyn Ryckman returned from furlough in 1952, Donald continued on in his studies at Los Angeles Pacific College. Harold and Evalyn spent a little time in Asunción where the Veseys and the Hankinses were now working along with Esther Harris and Betty Reynolds. Then they moved to Campinas. Don and Elda Rose Bowen, who had been in Campinas for language study for most of a year, now moved to the Sao Paulo mission apartment. I went to the mountains of Campos do Jordao to take over a new work Helen had started.

While Harold was still in language school, he frequently consulted with nationals and missionaries regarding the location for a Bible school and seminary. Both groups favored a rural setting. We reasoned that

77

students from interior churches would be more willing to return to such areas if they did not become accustomed to city living. Also, we knew that the cost of land and building in the city would be prohibitive.

Harold wrote Dr. Lamson on November 22, 1952:

"This letter concerns property for the seminary. . . . We feel that we have found just what we need.

"It is located near the new paved highway being constructed between Sao Paulo and Belo Horizonte. . . . On the new highway it is only twenty-five kilometers out of Sao Paulo. The climate is good, being one thousand feet higher altitude than Sao Paulo. More sun, but cooler. It contains about sixty-five acres . . . consists of two canyons and surrounding mountainsides covered with natural forest. I presume there are ten acres on which we can build. . . . There is a road right to the gate. . . . Electricity is also available. . . .

"The property is an estate. The two sons are anxious to sell and will negotiate for eight thousand dollars. It may not last long at this price. Other land is much higher. I hope this is not too sudden a shock to you. I don't know just how this will work out with the budget."

The letter was well received in Winona Lake, but there was no money for such a project. However, God was preparing a way. Dr. B. H. Pearson, a Free Methodist minister, who had been in Brazil under another board, was in Michigan as the guest speaker at Spring Arbor College. He presented the challenge of open doors in Brazil. The Holy Spirit began to speak to faculty and students. A committee went to Winona Lake to discover the most pressing need of our mission in Brazil. Just at that time, the missionary secretary had received a telegram from Brazil concerning the urgency of finding some way to purchase the Mairipora property. Spring Arbor accepted the challenge!

This project, taken on by Spring Arbor, sparked on

that campus and in area churches, a dynamic interest in missions that lasted for several years. The school raised the money for the land and also for several buildings — a total investment of about seventy-five thousand dollars. The project was especially appropriate for the college since Don and Elda Rose Bowen were graduates of Spring Arbor and since Don was to be the president of the new "Spring Arbor of Brazil."

To further strengthen the tie between Spring Arbor and Brazil, the college sent the student body president, James Chapman, to South America. He lived with the Ryckmans in Campinas and then in Vila Galvao for a few months.

Harold met with many delays in getting the title to the new property. There were other trying circumstances connected with the importing of their used car from the United States and the transfer of their personal effects from Paraguay. The following excerpts give insight into the type of situation with which many a missionary must learn to cope. On April 4, 1953, he wrote:

"I haven't gone over to Paraguay yet. . . . I sent my passport into Rio nearly six weeks ago. They requested it to study the possibilities of granting an import license for the car. I haven't received it back and cannot travel without it. I have gone to the Import Bank every two weeks. They keep saying . . . that it will eventually come.

"I am becoming rather impatient. . . . I may make a trip to Rio to see what it is all about. We are getting to the place where we shall be needing the car the worst way. We can get by while going to school here in Campinas, but when we get the property for the seminary we must have it. Please pray. . . ."

Then on June 30:

"We have finally received the Chevrolet. It arrived two weeks ago. . . . It is in just as good shape as the day I placed it in storage in 1952 in California.

"We have also received our baggage from Paraguay. In fact, the Chevrolet and the baggage arrived on the same day. This baggage shipment has been a headache. I left it with the exporter in Asunción last July. He promised to ship it out the very next week. He finally got it off two months later. He made out the shipping invoice by just guessing at the weight. When it arrived in Buenos Aires it weighed considerably less than it was billed. Hence, they assumed that part of it had been stolen. It took two more months to get this straightened out.

"Finally, the shipper in Buenos Aires sent the baggage to Santos, Brazil, on December 23, 1952. He sent the bill for the shipping back to Paraguay. Don Vesey secured the Argentine pesos and paid the exporter. The latter never paid the agent in Buenos Aires until April 18. Hence, he would not deliver the shipping documents to me until after that. When I received them April 20, my passport was tied up trying to get the import license for the car. On May 18 I got my passport and could proceed to get the baggage out of customs.

"Upon doing this I was informed that I had had just six months to bring my things in as 'baggage.' It was now in the category of 'merchandise' and would require an import license. . . . For two weeks we worked in every way possible to keep them from confiscating the whole thing. At last, by paying a heavy fine and full customs, we were able to get it.

"Frankly, I am ashamed that it has cost so much to get us moved over here from Paraguay. I have written these details to show that it was caused by things beyond our control. Don Bowen, mission treasurer, will be reporting the total cost. I think it will be about four hundred and fifty dollars. Too much — but I just couldn't do better."

It's easy to understand why Harold always told new missionaries to Latin America: "The first word you must learn is *paciencia* — 'patience.'"

In Harold's missionary report of that year he stated:

"Perhaps my most important achievement personally this year has been the conquering of the Portuguese language so as to be able to preach the gospel to the Brazilians. This is more important than one generally realizes. The foreign missionary who does not master the language of the country where he is working soon loses the respect of the national and thus limits his influence. . . . Spanish and Portuguese are so similar that it has been very difficult to differentiate and keep them entirely separate. . . . To my great satisfaction, I can now change back and forth without a lot of difficulty. I am hoping that time and practice will facilitate my efforts on this line."

At forty-three years of age Harold had tackled Spanish; at fifty he had taken on Portuguese. God enabled him to become fluent in both, though he had a Spanish accent in his Portuguese. Brazilian strangers, noticing his accent and his tall, angular physique, would often ask, "Senõr, are you a German from Argentina?"

Brazil Mission family, 1955, (1. to r.): Donald and Elda Rose Bowen, Harold and Evalyn Ryckman, Lucile Damon and Helen Voller

Japanese congregation at Lins

José Emerenciano, center, faithful colaborer for many years in Brazil

Donald and Elda Rose Bowen, Bobbie and Luanna, leaving
Brazil for furlough, May, 1955

Missionary Harold Ryckman looks across a beautiful section of sea and mountains outside Rio de Janeiro.

Dr. Reinaldo DeCoud presents first copy of Guarani New Testament to seminary; received by President James Mannoia, 1956.

Students and teachers in front of classroom building at Brazil seminary, 1961

Young lady works in front of the family farm home in Brazil.

A Brazilian farm home

Above and below right:
In Egypt with Executive Board of World Fellowship, 1963

Harold Ryckman at Asia Area Fellowship in Hong Kong, 1965

Light and Life Crusade in Sao Paulo (l. to r.): Wesley and Mary King, Lucile Damon, Sylvia Harden, John and Bobbie Hendricks, Clancy and Doris Thompson, Roy and Doris Kenny, James and Florence Mannoia, 1966

Lucile and Harold Ryckman in Sao Paulo, 1971

Chapter 12

Builder
and Administrator

What do you do when the Sunday school being held in a tent on rented land is bursting out at the seams? That was a question plaguing Helen Voller in Campos do Jordao. Harold came up with an ingenious solution. He wrote Dr. Lamson in September, 1953:

"It seems that the tent which Helen has been using for the Sunday school is too small now. It is only twelve by sixteen feet, and there are sixty in it at times.

"So, we have a plan to build a collapsible tabernacle ... which can be made in panels of six by eight feet and be bolted together. This can be enlarged later by simply adding more panels. It would be useful wherever we might be. We have permission from the owner of the house where Helen lives to put up such a building and to move it if we wish.... Don Bowen and I will build it, possibly right here in Sao Paulo, and have it shipped up to Campos do Jordao by truck. I have estimated the cost at three hundred and fifty dollars."

By the time Harold and Don had the panels ready, Wesley Hankins and his family had come from Paraguay for a vacation, and the three men did the assembling up at the mountain station. It proved to be just what was needed, not only there but in many other locations. Through the years, several of these portable tabernacles have been used in the Brazilian conference for new congregations until they were able to build permanent church buildings. Baptist missionaries asked permission to borrow the plans and they, too, found it very helpful.

Harold was a capable architect, director of construction, skillful cabinetmaker, and a careful businessman. While living in Vila Galvao, he directed the first construction on the seminary property near Mairipora. On September 30, 1954, he wrote to Dr. Lamson:

"It has taken longer than anticipated to finish the residence. . . . We will be moving out there in another week. It has been difficult to find men capable of doing finish work. I am doing all the cabinetwork myself.

"The cost of the house will be a bit less than sixty-five hundred dollars. This also includes garage, walls, and fence. There is stone facing on the fireplace and front porch. It shows what can be done when one does not have to work through an engineer and follow restrictions imposed by the city. . . . I have a fine constructor to help me, . . . efficient and above all, honest, I want, if at all possible, to keep him for future building."

Fortunately, he was able to hold this excellent workman, Sr. Brandino, as foreman of all the construction work. A warm friendship and mutual respect developed between the two.

Within two years, another residence, a classroom building, and two dormitories were completed. A new entrance road was made to connect the property with Mairipora, on the other side of the mountain, cutting the distance to the village to one mile. Wells were dug, pumps installed, an old building remodeled for temporary kitchen and dining room. Classes opened in 1957. At that time I moved to the apartment made for me in the girls' dorm and took on teaching and other responsibilities. Donald Bowen, president of the seminary, had learned much from Harold about building. He directed the construction of the third faculty residence during Harold's second furlough.

Landscaping on the campus, under Elda Rose's direction, added to the surrounding natural beauty.

Azaleas, roses, hibiscus, and coleus hedges adorned the front yards. Fast-growing evergreens alternated with poinsettia trees along the entrance and inside roads.

Upon Harold's return, the next project was a beautiful structure housing a large kitchen, dining room, and veranda. He was overwhelmed with the finish work to be done before school opened. We were to have a bigger enrollment, and the old temporary building would no longer meet the need. God came to his rescue by sending Roy Kent, a skilled, experienced cabinetmaker. Roy and Delight, self-supporting lay missionaries from an independent church in California, were providentially led to our seminary and stayed with us four years.

In his superintendent's report Harold gave this testimony:

"The Lord is very precious to me these days when the pressure of the work is heavily upon me. I find in Him a constant supply of inspiration and strength. . . . He is my personal Saviour and Sanctifier and I am His forever!"

One of Harold's expressions when we were tackling a tedious and difficult task was, "Just keep gnawing away at it." That is what he did, though it was not easy at times. His report of 1955 indicated some of his frustrations in the midst of so much building responsibility:

"The real reason for missions is to get souls saved. We believe this has first place in our hearts, although it seems that our letters have so much of material content. In fact, at times the missionary cries out from the depths of his soul to be relieved from so much of the material. . . . But my job is to a large extent administering and directing the work."

As an administrator, Harold had a gift of inspiring confidence, giving encouragement, and helping to keep peaceful interpersonal relationships. The welcome mat was always out at the Ryckman house where Evalyn was a gracious hostess. Missionaries and nationals felt at ease. Above all, we knew that Harold would be a patient listener as we poured out our problems. If possible, a helping hand would be extended to meet the need.

He rejoiced when new, younger missionaries came to the field. He wrote, "We have our young couples and we love them. We want to do the best possible for them. . . ." The children of these couples lovingly called him "Uncle Harold." They knew they could count on him as their friend.

Just as we needed guidance and counsel, so Harold felt a similar need. We were all looking forward to a visit from the missionary secretary in 1956. When word reached us that he could not make the trip, Harold wrote:

"We are surely disappointed. Not only did I want to show you the work and projects that are finished, but also to explain personally on the spot my thoughts, plans, hopes, and aspirations for forward steps. . . . It is rather lonesome pushing out ahead and planning for years in advance. I feel I need counsel from higher up. But, many times our disappointments are His appointments, so we will accept it as such."

Dr. Misuki, in writing of Harold's contributions to the church, states:

"One [contribution] was that he organized the Free Methodist Church of Brazil. Up to 1948, the Free Methodist Church was poorly organized, but under his leadership it came to assume the more usual Free Methodist structure" (page 82).

After presiding at one of those early conferences, Harold wrote:

"We are making progress in orderly business sessions. These people have a tendency to want to talk all at once. I have been trying to teach them the rules of order for church business. We are still having difficulty to get the minutes written up correctly. But it all takes time."

The "conference" in Brazil at that time was actually a district of the Pacific Coast Japanese Conference in California — an arrangement that Nishizumi had been able to make when he visited the States. To bring about a change, the group took action to form a separate South American Provisional Conference with three districts: Japanese, Brazilian, and Paraguayan. Each district would have its own superintendent, and all would work in cooperation with the mission superintendent. A committee began to work on a constitution. This provisional conference came into being in 1954 when the Reverend Edmund Snyder, area secretary, was in Brazil to preside at the meeting.

Of the spiritual aspect of the church, Harold stated:

"We are trying to raise up a church in South America which is truly a Free Methodist Church in standards, practices, and ideals. Holiness is our theme, not only as a theory but primarily as a practice in everyday living. . . . We are using every opportunity to preach the experience. It is bringing results and there is a vital quickening in many of the churches."

He kept in close touch with Paraguay by correspondence and frequent trips. He wrote on July 13, 1954:

"Evalyn and I have just returned from Paraguay. We were there from June 17 to July 10, three weeks of joyous, hard work. In the main, things are going better. . . . The arrival of electricity and the putting into operation of the water system have greatly improved living conditions."

By this time, the orphanage had been phased out. Most of the girls, now mature young women, had found places in the outside world. The few who wished to prepare further in the new Bible school lived in the homes of the missionaries. The orphanage buildings were transformed into residences.

Wesley Hankins directed the Bible school, while Donald Vesey led in the evangelistic aspect. Betty Reynolds carried on the clinic program. Both Esther Harris and Betty helped in new outstations and daily vacation Bible school work. In 1955, Esther announced her engagement to Dr. Reinaldo Decoud and her resignation as a full-time missionary. Previous to this she had talked the matter over thoroughly with Harold, who wrote Dr. Lamson:

"I could not conscientiously advise Esther against making this decision. This man is really very exceptional. He is perhaps the most outstanding layman in Paraguay. He is known and highly respected in many other Latin American countries. He is a professor in the state university, a credited psychologist, and within a year of getting his M.D. Also, he is president of the Central Committee of Evangelicals, a member of the Brethren Church, and has taught for two years in our Bible school. In short, Esther could not have found a finer man anywhere."

Though Dr. Decoud was involved in all of the above-mentioned activities, his chief goal was to translate the Bible from the original languages into the Guarani. To this end he had learned Hebrew, Greek, and Aramaic and had started to work on the project.

In Harold's report as superintendent in July 1956, he stated:

"This year represents just ten years of our mission in this field. While a great deal more should have been accomplished, we are reporting a little more than six hundred members. We have probably two thousand adherents to our churches. These ten years have been filled with hard work, tears, and many disappointments. . . . However, we are in a place where we can go ahead with more confidence and perhaps make much better gains.''

The total membership more than doubled in the next four years, reaching nearly thirteen hundred in 1960. Though the greatest growth was in the Japanese churches, there was a new outreach among the Brazilians with the coming of more missionaries. The Reverend and Mrs. Wesley King started a new church in Mairipora which the Reverend and Mrs. Clancy Thompson carried on when the Kings left on furlough. The Mirandopolis church outgrew its facilities under the pastorates of the Reverend and Mrs. Clarence Owsley and the Reverend and Mrs. John Mizuki. The Holiness Movement of Canada united with the Free Methodist Church in 1959. Their missionaries in Brazil, the Reverend Roy and Doris Kenny, became a part of our mission. In Paraguay the growth was slower, and this was of real concern to Harold.

Chapter 13

New Horizons in Paraguay

An international agreement opened an unexpected door for evangelism in Paraguay. In 1957, Japan promised a large loan to the little underdeveloped country. Paraguay was to repay the greater part by permitting a resettlement program, accepting approximately five thousand Japanese immigrants a year. When the immigration was underway, our church in Sao Paulo felt a responsibility to take the good news to the new settlers.

Up to this time our churches in Paraguay had all been within a radius of twenty-five miles of Asunción. In 1960, our missionaries, the Reverend and Mrs. Ernest Huston, moved from the capital three hundred miles south to Encarnación, an area receiving about three thousand Japanese annually. It was their plan to evangelize the Paraguayans and to offer their hospitality and transportation to the Japanese workers making trips over from Brazil.

Harold wrote Dr. Lamson from Encarnación on May 30, 1961:

"I have been here in Paraguay for two weeks visiting in the Japanese colonies. . . . The superintendent of the Japanese section of our conference, Mr. Sakuma, and I began our work in northern Paraguay, just across the border from Brazil, in Pedro Juan Caballero where there are colonies. . . . I did the preaching and Sakuma interpreted. I would prefer that he preach directly in

Japanese, but he always insists on doing it this way. . . . The whole colony is open to the gospel. We count ten families, representing at least fifty people, who can be considered Christians. . . .

"On Saturday of that week we flew to Asunción, arriving at 6:30 P.M. Since Ernie Huston had announced services in Encarnación and in the colonies for Sunday, we jumped into his Volkswagen and started out at 8:00 P.M. to go four hundred kilometers over poor roads. We arrived at 5:00 A.M. We had motor trouble on the way — burned a hole through one piston, ruining not only the piston but also the cylinder. Parts are not available here at present. They are on the way from Germany and expected within fifteen days. . . .

"The Japanese colonies in and around Encarnación are a mission field in themselves. . . . These immigrants come equipped with farming implements . . . tractors, jeeps, etc. . . . They are opening up the forest in a systematic manner, cutting roads, laying out the land in surveyed plots for each family, helping them to know what and how to plant. . . . In each colony we have homes where we can hold services regularly. Altogether, we preached six times.

"My impression is that this is one of the best opportunities for doing missionary work and seeing results in the saving of precious souls. . . . These are new immigrants, having left the old world with their old religions behind. They are open to the gospel now. After they become established in the country and are prospering materially, they will not be so susceptible to the gospel.

"We must get a full-time Japanese pastor in here as quickly as possible. We do not know just where we can find him as yet, for all of our pastors seem to be indispensable in their present places. But we are praying. . . ."

Within four months the answer to prayer had come, and Minoru and Yoko Tsukamoto were on their way to

Encarnación. I knew Minoru well and have often heard him tell of his early life in Japan. He was born in the home of a Shinto priest and his mother was a priestess. In his childhood he lived in constant fear of offending their many gods. While working as a radio operator in Tokyo during World War II, he experienced great hunger, both physically and spiritually. One day after the war he went out to buy food with his few coins. Passing a bookstore he felt a sudden, strong urge to enter. There he saw a New Testament for the first time in his life and bought it. The words began to feed his hungry spirit. A few months later he entered into a personal relationship with Jesus Christ. I have heard him say, "I used to be Mr. Hungry; now I am Mr. Satisfied!"

But how did Minoru get to Brazil and later to Paraguay? After his call to the ministry he attended Asbury Seminary in Wilmore, Kentucky. One of his good friends there was a student from Brazil, John Mizuki. Obeying the Lord's direction, Minoru went to Brazil. He taught English in our seminary, cataloged the library books, and evangelized the Japanese in the area — often walking miles to do so. Then he joined the Free Methodist Church and pastored a new church in the state of Parana.

Harold wrote Dr. Lamson on October 10, 1961:

"Our man for Paraguay is Minoru Tsukamoto. He is proving a very valuable man in our work. . . . He and his wife came to our home and lived with us for two months while they were getting their documents together. . . . They went to Paraguay about October 1 and plan to continue there as long as we want them. For their transportation we used the money reserved for a Japanese pastor from Brazil to visit in Paraguay. We had no money for their salary. However, I gave my 'superintendent's bonus' of one hundred dollars toward this; Mr. Huston is giving a large part of his tithe; and others are helping them through the rest of the year.

"We feel that Mr. Tsukamoto is the finest pastor we could have found. He was in Japan during and after the war and understands the postwar Japanese psychology. He is well prepared to answer the questions these people will raise regarding the Christian religion. . . . We want to stand back of this man."

The Tsukamotos are still in Encarnación, living in the house once occupied by the Hustons. Hundreds have found Christ through their ministry. One dedicated couple, the Sakais, took the responsibility for the little church in the Alto Parana colony. They were the victims of a cruel and horrible murder in 1969. But this did not stop the church. However, the rigors of pioneer agriculture, low prices for produce, and poor marketing conditions have caused many of the converts to move away, often to Argentina. Undaunted, the Tsukamotos have continued to seek and find the lost. A church has also been established in Pedro Juan Caballero in northern Paraguay.

And now the Pacific Coast Japanese Conference of southern California is helping to support a missionary in Argentina, Shonori Sugiyama. He came to the United States from Japan as a short-term agricultural worker. Through one of the men of the Free Methodist Church he was led to Christ. Then he returned to Japan to prepare for the ministry. In the early seventies he and his wife went to Paraguay and worked for a time with the Tsukamotos. In 1977 they began a work in Florencio Varela, a suburb of Buenos Aires.

*　　*　　*

After Harold's homegoing I received a letter from Minoru Tsukamoto. He said:

"Your letter came with the sad news. It is very hard for Yoko and me to express our deeply felt sudden shock. We have lost our 'Dad.'

"At the beginning of my life in Brazil more than

twenty years ago, I was disgusted by some of the conditions I found, and oh, how many times I poured out my feelings before Harold! I even told him that I would go back to the States. Patiently, he would listen to me. Looking back on those days, I see him as God's instrument to save me from 'falling apart' spiritually.

"Yoko and I remember very well that he and Dona Evalyna were the ones who helped us lay a solid Christian foundation for our life together. We will forever be thankful to them. And we are thankful to the Lord for his faithful ministry both in Paraguay and in Brazil. The Japanese church in Paraguay remembers him with much affection, for he was one of those who labored to let the church be born here."

Chapter 14

World Fellowship Secretary

The decade of the sixties was a time of upheaval, ferment, and change in the world. Our mission, seminary, and church in Brazil were not exempt. Harold gave stable leadership during the first years of that period. His new work with the World Fellowship took him away in the middle of 1962. This was a real loss to our Brazil-Paraguay area.

After a long hospitalization, Helen Voller returned to the States in January 1960. For five years she had carried a heavy load in the leadership of the Christian day school in Mirandopolis. Harold took steps to nationalize the school more completely.

Health problems beset him in his own home that year. Evalyn had become bedridden. She had considerable heart pain, caused probably by the hardening of the coronary artery. With the competent help of a Christian Brazilian girl, Jeronima Nascimento, in the Ryckman home, Harold was free to fulfill his commitments.

We were having a particularly stormy time in the seminary in 1961. There were twenty-five students. Those studying in the two-year Bible course were very cooperative, but some in the seminary level became discontented, vocal agitators; and among other things, they were advocating moving the school to Sao Paulo.

In his July 1961 superintendent's report Harold wrote:

"As I look back, I have a feeling that the greatest work of the past year was holding the ship steady and on course. Our missionaries have been working in Brazil and Paraguay for fifteen years. We now have eighteen fully organized churches, together with more than fifty annexes. . . . There are more than fifteen hundred members, thirteen ordained national pastors, eighteen licensed local preachers, and a good number of other lay workers. The ship has put out to sea and is going places. However, the agitation of the world ferment and discontent has roughed up the sea, and we have encountered stormy weather. We have had to pay strict attention to the guidance of the ship and not only keep the people on board but also keep the ship headed in the right direction. . . . It has taken a lot of indoctrination, scriptural teaching, and prayer to keep these people on board; but up to now, no one has fallen overboard. . . .''

In a letter to Dr. Lamson a month later regarding the problems of the seminary, Harold's concluding paragraph was:

''This is weighing heavily upon me these days. I want God's plan. If I am wrong, I want to be corrected. All of us are praying for divine direction. . . .''

The Bowens and I were scheduled to leave on furlough in early December of 1961. Their term had been six years and mine seven. But the death of Don's sister speeded up their departure.

Harold wrote on November 4, 1961:

''With the Bowens leaving on short notice and with Lucile leaving soon, together with the fact that all the principal leaders of our conference will be attending the Latin American Area and the World Fellowship conferences right at the beginning of the year and just before our own annual conference, we are very shorthanded, here, to say the least, right at a very crucial time. We were working day and night to get things done ahead of time, so as to avoid any more problems than are inevitable at the last moment. But we are making out OK, I believe."

The Kings would not be returning from furlough until the first of the year. The Thompsons, who had been pastoring the Mairipora church and teaching in the Bible school, now had extra heavy burdens upon them with the rest of us leaving. This is often the situation when missionary colleagues go on furlough.

In early January, Harold Ryckman and John Mizuki were in Florida among the delegates to the first Latin Area Fellowship. From there they went to Greenville, Illinois, to the first section of the organizing conference of the World Fellowship of Free Methodist Churches. With the great upsurge of nationalism all over the world, along with the rapid growth of our churches outside the United States, there was an urgent need to implement the aim of Free Methodist missions "to establish self-supporting, self-governing, and self-propagating churches as quickly as possible." Our General Conference, not the Missionary Board, had ordered these meetings.

National church leaders from all our mission areas sat down with delegates from North America, together with our bishops, to plan how to present Christ more effectively to a lost world. The Holy Spirit gave them real fellowship. One delegate from Africa said, "I forgot that I was black." The delegation unanimously approved a constitution. Harold Ryckman was chosen to be the first Executive Secretary to carry forward the decisions of the World Fellowship Board. The book *To Catch the Tide* by B. S. Lamson gives a comprehensive picture of the events preceding and during these conferences. The following quotations from that book give more of an idea of the scope of the work:

"The widely scattered churches around the world need a vehicle for the exchange of personnel, organizational ability, material and spiritual resources. . . . The members of the Fellowship are the general conferences and full conferences of mission origin and the area fellowships. . . . The World Fellowship is to cooperate with the bishops in assisting provisional conferences to achieve full conference status" (pages 95, 97).

Again Harold was being called upon to pioneer an uncharted field. Before he could set up his office in Winona Lake, he naturally had to return to Brazil. Mizuki tells about their trip. The plane from New York to Rio de Janeiro was delayed in leaving and the airline put them up in a luxurious New York hotel. That night Harold said, "John, I have never stayed in a hotel like this, but since it is only once in a lifetime, I think God will forgive us." As John commented, that was typical of Harold's simple life-style.

In June, the Ryckmans and their Brazilian "daughter," Jeronima, transferred their residence to Winona Lake. During the next three years Harold traveled extensively to visit the younger churches abroad. He spent hours helping the various provisional conferences prepare their constitutions to be submitted to the General Conference. Where there had been only three full conferences of mission origin in 1960, there were ten by 1964. Recognition by the mother church of the coming of age of its spiritual offspring contributed greatly to mutual understanding and to lessening of tensions. Through the promotion of cooperative projects, a great world concern gripped the churches in other lands.

In writing of the results of the World Fellowship Organizing Conference, one South American leader said:

"Decisions made at that time resulted in the South America Conference gaining the status of a full annual conference in January of 1964. This epoch-making event took place when Bishop Edward John declared solemnly at the assembly that the constitution had been approved by the Board of Administration and that from that moment we were starting as a new full conference. It was a high moment of emotion to all the ministers and lay delegates.

"The first result of our new status was evidenced when we sent, for the first time in our history, two delegates — one ministerial and one lay — to the General Conference in Winona Lake. This new status gives us new initiative.... This means more progress and more maturity in our work."

At the commencement in June of 1963, Los Angeles Pacific College awarded the doctor of divinity degree to Harold, lauding him for "his exemplary and dedicated leadership in promotion and development of the world Christian community."

To Harold this was a most unexpected recognition.

In October of 1965, Harold and Evalyn were still living in Winona Lake, though making plans to move shortly to Ontario, California. The organizing work of the World Fellowship was largely completed, and the Commission on Missions had asked for Harold's release to permit him to give full time as Area Secretary for Latin America. During the evening banquet of the fall board meetings, Evalyn became ill. The following day, Harold stayed by her side and had the doctor come to the home. The doctor found no cause for alarm; but in the early evening, Evalyn went to be with her Lord. Donald came at once and was a great comfort to his father. After the memorial service in the Winona Lake church, Donald flew back to California to complete the arrangements for the burial in Pomona. Harold made the long trip to California alone, accompanying the body of the one who had been his faithful companion for thirty-eight years.

Chapter 15

Latin America Area Secretary

The Free Methodist Church has work in Brazil, the Dominican Republic, Haiti, Mexico, Puerto Rico, Paraguay, and Argentina. In addition, there are churches among people of Hispanic origins in various cities of the United States. The Pacific Coast Latin America Conference has close ties with the church in Mexico. As Area Secretary, Harold was to give assistance to the churches and conferences in Latin America. He also served as liaison between the Latin America Fellowship, the Missionary Board, and the new General Missionary Secretary, Dr. Charles Kirkpatrick.

In the bleak winter days of December 1965, Harold made another lonely trip to California, pulling a small U-Haul trailer containing all his worldly goods. He set up his office and living quarters in the smallest apartment in the Ontario, California, Mission House. Kate Leininger, retired from China, and the Stanley Lehmans from Africa were in the other apartments.

Several changes had taken place in the Latin area, especially in Brazil. The Bowens had continued on furlough without salary and had accepted the pastorate in Sylmar, California. For health reasons, Helen Voller was unable to return to the field. I completed the master of arts program at the Wheaton Graduate School of Theology in mid-1963.

When I returned to Brazil to resume my teaching, I found an environment very different from the one I had

113

left. The seminary had moved to rented quarters in Sao Paulo. Seminary studies were offered in the morning, while classes on the Bible school level were scheduled at night. Though Brazil was still experiencing widespread communist agitation, our own school was calm. A sister seminary had been forced to close because of disruptive conditions in the student body.

The conference board of administration in Brazil and the Missionary Board had come to the conclusion that it would be wise to experiment with the city location. Our city work was growing much faster than the rural areas. Many young people in the city churches wanted to attend but needed employment. Also, it was proving difficult to secure part-time Brazilian teachers for the Mairipora location. The property there continued to be used for camps and conferences and for some missionary residences.

Dr. James Mannoia and his wife, Florence, had been appointed to Brazil in 1962. Dr. Mannoia, a former professor at Spring Arbor College, became president of the seminary. Other faculty members were the Reverend Wesley King, dean, and his wife, Mary; the Reverend John Mizuki; and Dr. Yoshikazu Takiya, who had just come back to Brazil after receiving his doctorate at Drew; and Dr. Reinaldo Decoud and his wife, the former Esther Harris, from Paraguay. Dr. Decoud was completing the translation of the New Testament from the original language into Guarani and needed to be away from his multiplicity of duties in Paraguay. Their two years with us met a great need at a crucial time.

Attendance at the seminary began to increase significantly, especially the night classes. In Sao Paulo, almost a fourth of the people, including young teens, were studying at night. Young people and adults from our churches and other denominations registered for classes. The seminary was well known in evangelical circles. Extension classes in our churches were organized to

114

prepare more laymen for their Christian service and witness.

The Brazilian section of the church was entering a phase of expansion. Portable tabernacles had been erected on land bought by the congregations in at least seven places. Roy Kent, at his own expense, came back from California for a few months to help with the construction of the tabernacles. Missionaries Roy Kenny and Clancy Thompson teamed up with a Brazilian evangelist in Crusades. Doris Kenny and Doris Thompson held Bible schools for the children. Wesley and Mary King were pastoring a new congregation in Vila Bonilha. Dr. and Mrs. Mannoia had started a Japanese Nisei (second generation) congregation in Portuguese.

To evangelize in these new locations, a Volunteers In Service Abroad (VISA) crusade team came to Brazil in July 1966 under the leadership of Donald Bowen. Dr. Harold Ryckman, the Area Secretary, also came to participate. Crusaders and missionaries often arranged it so that it was necessary for Harold to sit beside me at the dining table. After the Crusades, Harold stayed in Brazil for a few weeks.

On a beautiful spring day in September, the Thompsons invited Harold and me to go with their family to the Mairipora campus for a picnic. The sky was its deepest blue. Azaleas were in bloom and the fragrance of orange blossoms filled the air. That afternoon Harold asked me to become his wife. Both of us knew it was God's will. Never once in the eleven succeeding years did we ever doubt it. We planned a December wedding in Winona Lake.

Our missionary family and the national Christians indicated their genuine happiness with our decision. The missionary children had a lot of fun over the fact that "Uncle Harold" had to ask for car keys from one of their dads in order to take his fiancée home!

All too soon, Harold left for Winona Lake to attend the

115

board meetings. From there he went to Haiti and the Dominican Republic. I stayed in Brazil until December to finish out the school year. Harold wrote me on November 25:

"The countdown reads twenty-one now. Just three more weeks and we will be *one*. Praise the Lord! I am so happy about it all. I feel that I am living just in the reverse of old Job. The Lord hath taken away and the Lord hath given, blessed be the name of the Lord! Truly He is so good to us, isn't He? I feel so certain and secure in what we are doing. To be in the center of the will of the Lord and, at the same time, have exactly what you want is really wonderful." In another letter he said, "I think we will be a good team."

It was a joyous time as we took our vows in the Winona Lake Church with Dr. Lamson by Harold's side and Elda Rose Bowen by mine. Bishop Myron Boyd, chairman of the Commission on Missions, and Dr. Charles Kirkpatrick officiated. The soloist was Mary King. The tightly-knit missionary family becomes very apparent at such special times. Among the relatives present were Harold's son and his granddaughter Teri. Because his grandson, Russell, was ill, Don's wife and Russell could not come. Don later told me that he had been secretly hoping that "Dad would go back to Brazil and get Lucile." All of the Ryckman family took me into their hearts, and I have them in mine.

During the three succeeding years our work was mainly in the Pacific Coast Latin America Conference, in Mexico, and Haiti. Harold always cheerfully accepted the assignments that came to him. We lived in a little travel trailer while teaching in the Bible school in Hermosillo and also while preparing the VISA Crusade in Ensenada, Baja California. He would sometimes say, "A husband and wife have to be good friends to live long in such small quarters." We were the best of friends! He was "as

116

comfortable as an old shoe'' to be with, wherever it might be. We shared a deep love and mutual respect.

An emergency developed in Haiti in the summer of 1968 when Roy Kenny, who had been transferred there from Brazil, became very ill with typhoid. After the initial recovery, the doctor advised an immediate furlough to Canada. Roy's next project had been to build another church. This one was to be in Gonaives, on the Caribbean, one hundred miles north of Port-au-Prince. Harold and I went to ''fill the gap.'' We could not get away until October. The church needed to be ready before Christmas for a VISA Crusade from Dearborn, Michigan, the church that furnished the money for the building. Time-wise it looked impossible to Harold. He promised to do his best, and the people in Dearborn promised to pray.

Living conditions were the most primitive we had ever experienced. The only house we could find to rent was by the Mapou church, five miles out in the country from Gonaives. We paid ten dollars a month. There was no water, no electricity, no windows nor screens, only wooden shutters. Flies were so bad at noon that we had to keep the platters of food covered. A dear Christian lady, Madame Raul, carried water for us in a pail balanced on her head. But there was natural beauty all around on which to feast the eyes. It was a delight in the morning to hear the elementary school children in our church reciting their lessons and at night to hear the choir practicing. Especially beautiful was the ''Alleluia'' they prepared for Christmas.

With the Lord's help, Harold found a Christian Haitian, Brother Gabriel, to work alongside him as interpreter. Harold knew neither Creole nor French. Gabriel spoke both languages, as well as English and Spanish. Bringing with him his young daughter Minerva and his son Neptune, he rented a tiny house near us for the duration. When we finally left Mapou, Neptune begged to go with us.

Many of the building materials came by ship from Port-au-Prince to Gonaives. Rock for the foundation was crushed with a hand sledge. The ten doors were handmade from rough-hewn logs. In the first weeks, the heat was so oppressive that Harold could not use socks inside his shoes. But in spite of all the handicaps, the cement block walls went up far faster than he had imagined possible.

Most of the workmen were Christians from the local congregation which had been meeting in an overcrowded store building. Harold arrived at the construction one morning to find a good worker ready to quit. After he had poured out his complaint against a fellow worker who had, he felt, insulted him, Harold said, "But, brother, you could forgive him, couldn't you?" Tears came to the worker's eyes. Within minutes he was back on the job. There were times when one of the men would start singing a gospel song and others would soon join in. It sounded like a camp meeting!

Dearborn had sent three workers, Mr. and Mrs. Ernest Kelly and Mr. Gerald Rice, to help for two weeks in the early days of the construction. Then at just the right moment in December, three skilled workmen, Ernest Ivers and his son Cappie, and Jerry Hinkle, arrived from our Vincennes, Indiana, church. Their assistance with the finishing lifted a heavy load from Harold.

All was in readiness for the dedication on the Sunday *before* Christmas! The church, forty by eighty feet, accommodated five hundred persons. On that wonderful jubilee day more than six hundred were inside and out to praise the God of miracles who had made it all possible! Harold preached the dedicatory sermon.

After the crusade, we moved to the comfortable mission house in Port-au-Prince for a few weeks. Within two days Harold came down with dengue fever. The Haitians call it the *bone-acher* sickness. There is no medicine to give relief. The patient just has to have *paciencia*.

Harold occasionally remarked, "I wouldn't have the experience in Haiti taken out of my life for a million dollars! Neither would I want to do it again for a million!"

Chapter 16

Return to South America

Harold was sixty-eight years old and nearing retirement when a pressing need arose in Brazil in 1970. Two of the missionary families, the Mannoias and the Thompsons, were soon to leave the field indefinitely. The Howard Snyders and the Wesley Kings were to go on furlough a little later. The Missionary Board asked Harold if we would be available to fill the gap for a year or two. He knew the demands in Brazil would be taxing, but again he did not shrink back. For years his policy had been to enter the doors he was sure God opened. I was in perfect agreement.

We left in June, stopping on the way for two delightful days in Colombia with the Biddulphs and the Hankinses. As we flew southeastward over the vast Amazon forest, I asked the Lord to give us strength to face the many problems I knew were ahead. Immediately the Holy Spirit whispered, "Stand still, and see the salvation of the Lord" (Exodus 14:13). Both of us accepted this as *our* verse.

New sights met our eyes in Sao Paulo. There was a new freeway from the Congonhas airport, right through the center of the city. A new three-story seminary building had been constructed under Dr. Mannoia's administration. There was an enormously deep trench in the street at the front door of the school. A subway was to become a reality, and a station was to be just across the corner — ideal for the many commuting seminary students! Attendance at the seminary continued to increase.

121

Money from the sale of the Mairipora property had been reinvested in the new building and faculty residences. A handsome profit had made it possible to obtain a very favorable city location that otherwise would have been financially prohibitive. A group of doctors had purchased the other property for a hospital specializing in nervous disorders. At times Harold was severely tempted to wonder why God had so miraculously helped in the Spring Arbor project and then in so few years had changed the direction. He never brooded over such questions. He would put them "up on the shelf," as he expressed it, along with all the others. He knew that in God's time the answer would come. He did take comfort in the fact that valuable workers now in the full-time ministry had been trained at Mairipora and that seminary personnel had planted the church at the nearby town.

We also saw in Sao Paulo the impressive Mirandopolis church, started by John Mizuki. It was nearing completion with Clancy Thompson as pastor. This was on the original mission property adjacent to the first chapel-residence that Harold had built in 1947-48. The Mizukis were in California where John was a pastor in the Pacific Coast Japanese Conference and enrolled in the doctoral program at Fuller Seminary.

In Vila Bonilha, the Kings were getting plans underway for a sanctuary to replace the portable tabernacle. Several new Brazilian pastors were extending our work in outer areas. The Emerencianos were beginning a well-earned retirement. In the Japanese conference (Nikkei) there were new churches in Sao Paulo, though the overall growth had slowed down.

Within a month after our arrival, The Mannoias returned to the States, and Harold shouldered the responsibility of interim president of the seminary. He had strong support from Howard Snyder, the dean. I accepted teaching assignments.

The Thompsons returned to the homeland the end of

January. Clancy had been superintendent of the Brazilian conference as well as a pastor. At the request of the conference, Harold agreed to act as superintendent for just one year. Then there would be more national pastors ordained and eligible for election.

After conference we went to Asunción where Harold presided at their annual meeting. Many changes had taken place there, too. We stayed in the Huston home and were grateful that we no longer had to fight hordes of mosquitoes at night. The city had done something about that problem! In fact the whole city had a much more progressive look and atmosphere.

In the middle of the sixties, the clinic had closed and Betty Reynolds had been transferred to our work in the Dominican Republic. Asunción Christian Academy bought our original property in the late sixties. Lucy Huston had started this school when her own five children were youngsters. Instruction was in English and chiefly missionary kids of other denominations attended, though some Paraguayans also came. The sale necessitated relocating the church and a missions residence. The Reverend Timothy Shumaker, a first-term missionary, directed the new construction. The dedication took place the Sunday we were there.

Before we returned to Sao Paulo we had two days of wonderful fellowship with Pastor Minoru Tsukamoto and his family in Encarnación. They are real pioneer missionaries! A ferry trip across the wide Parana River to the Argentine town of Posadas permitted a glimpse of a modern city. I felt as if I were back in the States, except for the language.

In the following months, the conference superintendency, along with the seminary, weighed heavily upon Harold. Often the conference business meetings began at 10:30 P.M. when members were through with their day's work, their studies, or night teaching. Frequently they adjourned long after midnight. The problems kept coming up, as we had known they would. How many times we sought the Lord together asking for His solution. We also leaned heavily upon His promise, "Stand still, and see the salvation of the Lord."

One day in October 1971, both of us were sick with the flu. Harold was sitting on the edge of the bed with his head down. I said, "A penny for your thoughts."

"Do you really want to know? Well, I was talking to the Lord and telling Him that I am now on the homeward stretch. Just as a runner gives it all he has in the last lap of the race, so I want to give Him all I have."

When Conference was over in January 1972, the superintendency passed to the Reverend Expedito Calixto. Harold was more exhausted than I had ever seen him. We slipped away to the mountains at Aguas de Lindoia. During the week he worked on jigsaw puzzles of a thousand pieces. That was one of his best ways of relaxing.

Our students also carried heavy loads. For example, there was José V. in Harold's class on Pauline epistles. He worked in an office all day, then grabbed a sandwich and fought the crowds on buses for two hours to reach the seminary at 7:30 P.M. After classes he would reach his home in Vila Galvao about midnight. Almost all of the students had jobs and church obligations. That is the way of life in Brazil.

Fighting the traffic in Sao Paulo, now nearing ten million in population, is an experience in itself! Nationally manufactured cars, especially VW "bugs," clog the freeways and the narrow streets. Harold was an excellent driver, but we had scraped fenders four times in those two years. The insurance agent would shrug his shoulders and comment: "Oh, that is to be expected."

Pastors invited Harold to preach nearly every Sunday in their churches. Preaching was very dear to his heart, and as one Brazilian brother said, his sermons were always edifying. Because of a traffic tie-up we were almost

124

late getting to the Mairipora church one night. Pastor Azarias told us later that he had prayed for a message when he began to fear we would not arrive. Almost at once a scripture had come to his mind and an outline for it. To his amazement, it was the same basic sermon which Harold preached!

Every second Sunday of the month he preached in the Reverend Sukeichi Ono's church in Santana, on the north side of Sao Paulo. In September, that Sunday coincided with Harold's birthday. At the close of the service the leader said, "Rev. Ryckman, please stay with us a little longer this morning." The congregation was meeting temporarily in a large upstairs hall. The young people hurriedly pushed back the chairs, placed long tables across the auditorium, and served huge platters of food. Last of all, they brought a beautifully decorated birthday cake. It was a complete surprise and delight to Harold!

Further changes in personnel occurred in 1971. The Takiyas came back from the States where Dr. Yoshikazu had been teaching at Greenville College. He taught at the seminary and also served as the pastor of the Mirandopolis church. It continued to grow under his leadership.

Douglas and Beth Smith from Michigan, new appointees, arrived in 1971. Their little adopted biracial daughter, Kirsten, won her way in Brazilian hearts. "Here are Americans without race prejudice!" was a frequent comment. Brazil, of course, had been a melting pot with interracial marriages from her earliest history.

Howard and Jan Snyder left on a six-month furlough, planning to return about the time of our departure. The Kings would not be leaving until August. Along with his teaching, Wesley was working night and day to get the sanctuary completed where he was pastor. When they left, the Brazil mission was reduced to two couples.

Time drew near for our leaving Brazil in June of 1972. Pastors and laymen of the Japanese (Nikkei) and Brazilian conferences began to express their love and appreciation in special ways.

There were farewell dinners, teas, long-stemmed roses, gifts of artifacts, and visitors in our home. The Brazilian conference came together from the various churches on a Sunday evening for a meeting in Harold's honor. When we left, the crowd at the airport was unbelievable. With tears near the surface, we bade a fond farewell to these dear people we both loved so much.

Harold had become a bit anxious about a house for our retirement. He wanted to settle in California in the Ontario area. His aged mother lived there as well as his two brothers, Ernie and Russell. Donald, a school administrator in Manhattan Beach, was not too far away.

One day while yet in Sao Paulo, we had read in *Daily Light* the verse, "The Lord shall choose our inheritance for us." Immediately, Harold said, "That is right! We shall trust in Him." Another promise given to us about the same time was from Psalm 92: "The godly ... are transplanted into the Lord's own garden, and are under his personal care. Even in old age they will still produce fruit and be vital and green. This honors the Lord, and exhibits his faithful care" (Psalm 92:12-15, *The Living Bible*).

Shortly after we arrived in southern California, Harold's brother Russell took us to a quiet street to see a lovely two-bedroom house. We were able to purchase it at an unusually low price. Harold never ceased to thank God for His provision. He would say, "These are the exact square feet the Lord chose for us!"

We continued in deputation work for the Missionary Board. Harold was retired shortly before his seventy-first birthday. Dr. James Mannoia replaced him as Area Secretary.

"Retired by the Board, but not by the Lord," Harold continued to accept assignments. For three years we traveled with the trailer to teach for short periods in Mexico at the Hermosillo Bible school. The last time we were there, February of 1976, Harold said, "We must work closer to home. This long trip is becoming too heavy." So, he limited his activities chiefly to the local church in Upland. We started a Bible study in our home. He continued with committee work in the Pacific Latin American Conference. He was a member of that body.

In September 1976, a numbness came over his left side and never fully left him. We were so grateful to God that there had been no paralysis nor lessening of mental alertness. Then suddenly, in January 1978, a severe heart attack laid him low. In the seven weeks following he was in the hospital three different periods. His visitors were limited chiefly to family and ministers. Donald was often by his side. One day, with a big smile, Harold said to Sixto Tarin and Herbert Newland, "You men preach about getting a new heart. Now, I want you to tell me how to do it."

In typical manner, he did not complain about his illness but greeted visitors and nurses in his usual cheerful way. As I entered his room one morning, he said, with outstretched hand, "Here comes the gem of my heart!"

One night I said, "Honey, I stopped awhile at prayer meeting. The pastor asked for continued prayer for you. He also said that people in many parts of the world are praying for Harold Ryckman."

I shall never forget Harold's reply:

"When I think of that little 'squirt' milking cows on the farm in Chino, I cannot understand how he has people in other parts of the world praying for him."

Then he went on to say, "I have had time for much reflection these days. As I look back, I am so thankful to God. I do not know of anything I would want to change as far as major decisions go. I do not know about the future, but you know that I am ready to go."

We had four good days together at home with great hope for his recovery. Then in the early hours of February

21, I found that he had slipped away to a far better place. "Payday" had come for Harold Ryckman!

Jesus said, "I say unto you, There is no man that hath left house, or parents, or brethren, or wife, or children, for the kingdom of God's sake, who shall not receive manifold more in this present time, and in the world to come life everlasting" (Luke 18:29, 30).

PB 55

128

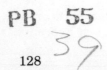

64504